M

M

Music in American Life

A list of books in the series Music in American Life appears at the end of this volume.

Crazeology

BUD FREEMAN

Crazeology

The Autobiography of a Chicago Jazzman

As Told to
Robert Wolf

With a Foreword by Studs Terkel

University of Illinois Press
Urbana and Chicago

This book is printed on acid-free paper.

Library of Congress Cataloging-in-Publication Data

Freeman, Bud, 1906–
    Crazeology : the autobiography of a Chicago jazzman / Bud Freeman,
  as told to Robert Wolf : with a foreword by Studs Terkel.
      p. cm.—(Music in American life)
    Bibliography: p.
    Includes index.
    ISBN 0-252-01634-3 (alk. paper)
    1. Freeman, Bud, 1906–   2. Jazz musicians—United States—
Biography.   I. Wolf, Robert.   II. Title.   III. Series.
ML419.F74A3   1989
788'.42'0924—dc19
[B]   89-4704
                                         CIP
                                         MN

For Roger Isaacs,
without whose support this book would
not have become a reality.

Contents

Illustrations follow page 46.

Foreword

Bud Freeman is a natural-born storyteller, no less than he is a natural-born jazz artist. It is hard to tell where his tenor sax leaves off and his easy flow of words begins. His music and his talk are of one piece; the delight is indivisible. If I were to choose a phrase to describe Bud's style as a musician and as a raconteur, it would be "twinkly elegance." Listeners, no matter what baggage they carry with them, feel lighthearted and unburdened. Readers of *Crazeology* will feel the same. Writer Bob Wolf turns out to have been the ideal colleague of Bud's.

This story of his life, simply told — it is oral; you can hear his voice and inflections in these pages — is one man's history of jazz. You really come to appreciate the true genius of Louis and Bix; of the human failings of others, equally renowned, and of Bud's own, of course. His honesty is that of a wide-eyed child. Fuse this sense of innocence and wonder to the worldly wisdom of someone who has seen it all and you have a portrait of Bud. At eighty-two he still has what Jane Addams once called the "unquenchable spirit of youth."

It is here in Chicago, of course, where his tale begins. It is here where he has returned, his home rediscovered, his first love rekindled. It is here where you might run into him sauntering along the Magnificent Mile, dapper in the British fashion. "I'm an Anglophile," he enunciates softly. Of course you smile; which is what he had in mind in the first place. His sense of humor, gentle, sly, yet so innocently offered, pervades this book. Recently, a Hamburg impresario invited him to perform at several German jazz festivals. Bud declined; travel is too exhausting these days. "But Herr Freeman," the man replied, "we have excellent hospitals in Germany."

Make no mistake, though; *Crazeology* is more than a lighthearted journey through romantic attachments, idiosyncratic colleagues, world travels . . . and very funny stories (I lost count of the number of times I laughed out loud). It is about the everlasting debt we owe the black jazz artists for enriching our lives. From the first glowing moment that Bud and his Austin High School buddies traveled to the South Side and heard young Louis with King Oliver and Bessie Smith and Earl Hines and Jimmie Noone, his life was transformed. And so was ours, whether we realize it or not. Bud's simple manner in describing the graciousness of his black mentors and of the black community puts to shame much of the shallow, "profound" commentary on race that we hear these confabulating days.

In short, Bud Freeman has offered us a lovely book, and I am eternally grateful to his late brother, Arny, an actor colleague of mine during our greening days, for having introduced me to Lawrence (Bud) Freeman. It was so many hard winters and soft summers ago, yet the memory is indelible. What's even more rewarding is that I can hear Bud perform—as well as ever—these days, around and about Chicago. So can you. Talk about good luck.

Studs Terkel

"Bud and the Boys"

Louis Armstrong thought Chicago was the greatest place for a young jazz musician to have been born, and for my money there never was or will be a better place than Chicago in the twenties. Young musicians had the best possible opportunity for learning about this music because we had most of the great jazz musicians living among us. We had wonderful clubs on the black South Side, where the likes of Louis, King Oliver, Jimmie Noone, Earl Hines, and Baby and Johnny Dodds gave us the greatest music lessons we could ever ask for. The South Side also had great singers of the caliber of Bessie Smith and Ethel Waters. On the white North Side we could hear Bix Beiderbecke, Ben Pollack, and half a dozen other greats.

It was not dull in Chicago in the twenties. Prohibition was on and the only places we could play the music we loved were the gangster-owned clubs and speakeasies. There were tensions in the town, and not just between the powerful criminals. Chicago was divided between blacks and whites, a town of terrible prejudice. In 1919, when I was thirteen years old, the tension exploded in some of the worst race riots of all time. The black population had grown rapidly during World War I, when the wartime industrial boom created thousands of new factory jobs. That black migration from the South brought with it not only factory hands but jazz musicians. In the late nineteenth century Chicago had been the fastest-growing city in the world, bustling and crass. In my youth it was still raw, still a young giant with belching steel mills and sprawling stockyards, the largest in the country. That was the town I grew up in, at a time when almost everyone played ragtime on their parlor pianos.

Chicago, not New Orleans, was the town that really cradled jazz. New Orleans, I think, spawned a kind of ragtime that developed into jazz in Chicago through the genius of King Oliver and Louis Armstrong. If anyone should get the credit for developing Chicago-style jazz, it should be Oliver and Armstrong, the men who developed the beat that will be with us forever.

I was born in 1906 in Austin, which in those days was a near west suburb of Chicago. My father, who was a garment cutter, was Jewish; my mother was a French-Canadian Catholic. I grew up with an elder sister, Florence, and a younger brother, Arny. Arny and I encouraged each other's artistic aspirations. From an early age he wanted to become an actor, and for a time I did too. It was not until I went to Austin High School and met the McPartland brothers that I found my calling. It was Jimmy and Dick McPartland, along with Frank Teschemacher, Jim Lannigan, and Dave North, who helped focus my ambitions on music. I did not have music lessons as a child, but I had grown up with it and had always loved it. My parents had an upright piano, and my mother and her four sisters and three brothers could all play and sing. We were always having parties, and I had the feeling that I knew everything about music when I was eight years old.

The less said about my early education, the better. I tried to avoid it at all costs and was graduated from grammar school to Austin High School simply on the basis of winning all eight track and field events at a YMCA meet the summer before high school. My teachers probably regretted their decision to pass me: I paid no attention to my high school studies either. I was anxious to get out into the world, as were my other friends.

We had a number of professional musicians attending Austin High, some of whom were in a band that played for dances every Friday afternoon after school. Dave Tough, who would become the greatest jazz drummer in America, or anywhere, was going with a girl at Austin, and he used to come over from Oak Park every Friday to visit and dance with her. Dave had the sharp collegiate look we admired—a Norfolk jacket, a striped tie, and a colored shirt. He and his girl were both great dancers.

Dave sat in one afternoon with the band, and a big crowd formed around him because he was a professional drummer, which was a big deal to all of us. I thrust my hand through the crowd and he shook it. He was so friendly and warm.

I did not see him again for a year. When we did meet I said, "You don't remember me, but you're Dave Tough, the famous drummer." He said, "Yes, I remember you. You're that kid I met at Austin High." He remembered me because I had been so enthusiastic about his drumming. He thought that I was a musician because I talked so much about music. I did because I had been so environed with it in my home.

Dave would become one of the big influences in my life. He introduced me to painting and literature. When I was about sixteen he called me up one day and said, "Bud, there's a wonderful French post-Impressionist being shown today by the name of Paul Cézanne. Would you like to go to the Art Institute?" Now I confess that I'd never heard of Cézanne, but I said, "I'd love to go." So I saw this painting, *The Fruit on the Table*. The piece of fruit was a sort of purplish green color, which made it seem to stick out from the table. I said to Dave, "I wish I could say something about this magnificent work," and Dave said, "That's the best thing you'll ever say about it." He hated the idea of words for art.

Dave also introduced great authors to me when I was very young and couldn't understand them. I remember we went to see *Macbeth*. I hadn't the faintest idea what Shakespeare was saying, but I loved the sound of the words and on the strength of that experience became a Shakespearean theatergoer. Later, at the instigation of the great cornetist Bix Beiderbecke, we got into listening to Debussy, Ravel, Stravinsky, Scriabin, Gustav Holst, Jacques Ebert, all the so-called modern composers of our childhood.

Jimmy McPartland, although he was a year younger than I, was already a professional musician at fifteen. His father was an alcoholic and a rough guy, and when Jimmy was young he took after him. Jimmy was a street fighter, or had been before I knew him. He was fast and strong, and he worked out. He was not only a boxer but the best golfer at Austin High. He could have been a professional athlete. He was good-natured, and although he still had a temper when I met him, I never saw him fight.

By the time he was fifteen Jimmy was drinking heavily and one day passed out in front of my house. I called my father and he and two others carried Jimmy inside and put him into my father's bed. My father loved Jimmy. I'll never forget him lecturing Jimmy the next day: "This is terrible what you're doing to yourself." Jimmy looked up at him and said, "Mr. Freeman, do you have a beer?"

As I said, it was at Austin High that I became good friends with Jim Lannigan, Dave North, and the McPartland brothers. There was a soda parlor called the Spoon and Straw that we used to frequent in 1922 during my sophomore year. It had a little wind-up Victrola and stacks of records and we would play them while we had our sodas and shakes. One day we found a record by the New Orleans Rhythm Kings in the stack and we put it on, not knowing what kind of band we were about to hear. Were we excited by it! We were used to hearing commercial dance music, but this sound was something else.

We were so excited by that first record that we decided that afternoon to become jazz musicians and form our own band, which Dick later named the Blue Friars. He got the name from the fact that the New Orleans Rhythm Kings played at a club called the Friar's Inn and recorded under the name of the Friar's Society Orchestra. Little did we know that we were all to become world renowned. I picked saxophone, Jimmy McPartland cornet, Dick McPartland banjo, Jim Lannigan bass tuba, Frank Teschemacher clarinet, and Dave North piano. The McPartlands convinced my father to buy me a saxophone and he took me downtown to Lyon and Healy, a music store on Wabash Avenue. That's where I got my first horn, a C-melody saxophone. When I got home I tried to play it but couldn't get a sound out of it. Not a noise. You can imagine how disillusioning that was because then, at sixteen, I thought I knew all about music.

Although I couldn't play the horn I still treasured it and was afraid I might mar it in some way. I would open the case, assemble the instrument, and look at it. After a while I would run my hands over the keys and try to play it. When nothing came out I would wipe it carefully with a cloth to remove my fingerprints and put it back in its case. Eventually I learned to squeeze several notes from it. I was a ballroom dancer and I had a beat in my body that I could play. Dick was very enthusiastic about the few notes I could play and he taught me some chords. I learned those before I could read music.

From the early days, and for many years thereafter, I went through periods during which I would not touch the horn for weeks at a time. I would seem to forget about it or get disgusted with it. Part of that was due to laziness. When my mother died—she died shortly after I got the C-melody—my father said, "You boys don't have to worry. You have the house. There will always be food for you. Go on and do what you want to do. Be happy. But make sure that what you do is what you want to do." Arny and I almost became a couple of bums, but he wanted to be an actor very badly and I wanted to play very badly and that's what saved us. Father gave us the support we needed to become artists, but by the same token that very support encouraged my laziness. If I had been forced to earn a living I would not have laid off the instrument as often as I did, and I would have taken more jobs. Young people take advantage of their parents if they are given everything they want. I was a spoiled brat, and so was Arny, but he was tougher. He worked very hard at being an actor but I didn't work as hard at being a musician. I wished that I were a musician more than I worked at becoming one.

Mother had been ill and living in a sanitarium a long time before she died, and we had gotten used to the idea that she was not going to be with us very long. I think she was thirty-six when she passed on. It really didn't affect me until years later, when I sort of broke down. I had always had feelings of guilt. I would say to myself, "I wish I'd been better to her." My mother and I were very involved with each other and quarreled a great deal. She really loved me more than Arny and Florence, or so Dad told me. She was an accomplished amateur actress and she and her brothers, as I said, all played piano and sang. I suppose it was her interests that led Arny and me into the arts. She never knew anything about my becoming a musician, but she would have been thrilled if she had.

Soon after our gang heard that first record of the New Orleans Rhythm Kings, I borrowed a pair of long pants and went with the McPartlands to the Friar's Inn to hear them. Most of the men in that band, including cornetist Paul Mares, trombonist George Brunis, and clarinetist Leon Rappolo, were from New Orleans, but Ben Pollack, the band's drummer, was from Chicago. It has been said often enough that this new type of music—jazz—was born in New Orleans. Although it's true that a lot of fine jazz artists came out of New Orleans, I don't think this music developed there as much as it did in Chicago. As I said, New

Orleans really developed a form of ragtime playing. If you listen to recordings of old New Orleans bands you can hear the difference between the music of the men who never left that town and those who came to Chicago. People must understand that although New Orleans gets a lot of publicity for its "jazz," it never supported its "jazz" artists in those early years. If musicians were any good they had to get out of there, and all the great players did. Most came to Chicago.

By the way, we didn't call this music jazz. I haven't the faintest idea where the name came from. We didn't use any musical categories. We just knew this was a new sound, and as we got on and began to understand it through the records of the New Orleans Rhythm Kings, Bill Grimm, a student at the University of Chicago, took us out to the Lincoln Gardens to hear King Oliver's Creole Jazz Band. After that we never went back to the New Orleans Rhythm Kings because when we heard the King Oliver band, we knew that we were hearing the real thing for the first time.

Almost all the white musicians who played this music listened to King Oliver's Creole Jazz Band. They learned to play their beat, which was also the beat of the great Harlem pianists Willie "The Lion" Smith, James P. Johnson, Luckey Roberts, and Fats Waller. Willie called it "the beat of the heart," and many of the young white players learned to play it.

I was seventeen in 1923 when I first went to the Lincoln Gardens. Aspiring white jazz musicians used to go there all the time, and the people there were wonderful. They paid no attention to us; they knew we were there to hear the music. The big, black doorman weighed about 350 pounds, and every time he saw us he would say, "I see you boys are here for your music lessons tonight." He knew. That was rather a sage thing for him to say because hardly any whites knew about this music.

The Lincoln Gardens was a nightclub, about the largest I've ever seen, a big square place that held several hundred people. It was very dark inside and always jammed. Since this was during Prohibition, patrons brought their own liquor, as they did to other clubs and dance halls. These places all served setups—ice and ginger ale. The Lincoln Gardens was strictly a black club, but they didn't keep us out. The bouncers and the waiters knew us.

The dancing, by the way, impressed me about as much as the music. I never saw people enjoy it so much. Today, men and women don't touch each other when they dance, but at that club, when the band played slow tempos, their bodies seemed to be glued together, as though they were trying to move through each other. They seemed to be so in love, and they were so graceful; there was never a clumsy dancer.

The evening's music started with stock orchestrations, not with jazz or blues. The band would set up and play a number that might run ten or fifteen minutes. They would play it from the top down, and then as the people became more enthusiastic about the music and things got moving, you could hear the floor monitor, who stood up front to one side of the stage, shout, "One mo' time, King!" meaning, "One more chorus." If people did not circulate around the floor he would say, "Get off that dime, man. Move on." These blacks did not have the money to go to a club or dance hall more than once a week, but they had a wonderful freedom of spirit when they felt this music. I didn't know a white man with money who had that spirit.

In those days most white people were badly educated. We were brainwashed into believing that blacks were inferior to us. When I say "we," that goes for whites all over the world. We were taught to look down on any race that wasn't white. But I never felt that way because my father didn't have any prejudice. When we were very young he used to say, "Always remember, boys, that everybody has a life to live and yours is not the only one." We were very lucky to be raised without prejudice.

Now here were these black people who were allowed no privileges. They were not allowed to come into our shops and cinemas, but we whites were allowed to go out to their community, where they treated us beautifully. I found their way of life equally as important as their music. It was not just their music that moved me but the whole picture of an oppressed people who appeared to be much happier than we whites who had everything. It was on the strength of this that I developed a love for them and their music and became a jazz musician.

I never heard better music than at the Lincoln Gardens. What a thrill it was! We used to go out on a Saturday night because we did not have to get up early the next day and go to school. But once in a while we would sneak out there on a weeknight and run into some important musician who was in town. There weren't many musicians in those days who knew about this music and this wonderful place with the King Oliver band. Lil Hardin, a piano player who later married Louis

Armstrong, was with that outfit. So were guitarist Johnny St. Cyr, trombonist Honore Dutrey, bassist Bill Johnson, clarinetist Johnny Dodds, and drummer Baby Dodds. Of course King Oliver and Louis were also in the band, both playing cc et. Baby Dodds, incidentally, was a very strong influence on Dave Tough. It's interesting that Dave would go on to influence bebop drummers—black and white—with a style of playing that was developed forty years before bebop was born.

The first time I saw Louis Armstrong was the first night I went out with the McPartlands, Dave Tough, and Frank Teschemacher to hear the Creole Jazz Band. We didn't even know Louis's name—he was an unknown—but when we heard him play we found out immediately who he was. We made a point of it. I knew at once that I was hearing a great master. Louis was *the* great American voice, a great genius, and his guide and idol was King Oliver.

When the Creole Jazz Band played, each chorus seemed to swing more than the previous one until every bit of tension in you seemed to leave your body. That was the power of this music. There was nothing else like it on earth. If you couldn't dance, it made you dance. But we weren't there to dance, we were there just for the music.

I usually went there with Dave Tough, Jimmy, Dick, Tesch, Bill Grimm, George Wettling, or Floyd O'Brien, and we'd always run into somebody we knew. Floyd, who became a fine trombonist, really loved and understood the music. But of all those who went there, Dave (and Bix Beiderbecke, whom I met later) knew more about it than anyone I knew at that time. There were other musicians, white dance musicians who never became names, who used to go down too. Students from Northwestern and the University of Chicago also went there.

Shortly after I first heard Louis I took a few lessons on the C-melody sax from Jimmy McPartland's father. I didn't like them because I wanted to play my own way, to play the rhythm that was in me. I wanted to express my love for King Oliver's and Louis's playing, but Jimmy's father was teaching me chromatic, major, and minor scales. Even with those lessons I didn't really learn to read music until I got a tenor sax, two years later in 1925.

I was slower at learning my instrument than the others were at theirs. They had all had musical training (Tesch, the McPartlands, and Jim Lannigan had all played violin). Jimmy has said that Tesch wanted to throw me out of our band because all I could do for a long time was play one note. I don't know if the story is true, I never heard Tesch say it, but he always seemed angry, and not just with me.

The next year, in the summer of 1924, I began my professional career. I was eighteen when I got my first job on the C-melody sax. Dave Tough got it for me. He had gotten a job playing a roadhouse in Sheboygan, Wisconsin, and wanted me with him. It was incredible because I could play rhythmic patterns but not a melody. Dave told the pianist who was hiring the musicians that I was the world's greatest C-melody sax player. The man said he wanted to hear me play, but Dave told him, "Bud Freeman's too great an artist to audition." This guy, whose name was Woods, was a pretty good boozer. He was in his forties, heavyset, and bald. He had been a vaudeville piano player.

The fellow who owned the place was an ex-prizefighter named Cibby Sands. He had swinging doors separating the bar from the eating and dancing areas. The clientele was mostly college kids from eastern schools and the University of Wisconsin. There was an Indian who used to come in almost every night and say to Sands, "Me beat you." They used to wrestle for drinks. They'd be on the floor, rolling around, and the Indian was so drunk all the time that he always lost.

The place had a long waxed bar, and some drunk way down at the end of it would say, "Hey, Cibby, how about another bourbon?" Sands would slide a large shot glass full of whiskey down the bar and almost invariably it would fall off but he would keep sliding them until one reached its destination. He also had a slot machine that took fifty-cent pieces, and drunks would pour money into it all night. Fifty cents was a lot of money to me, but on several occasions I played it and a few times hit the big one for about fifty dollars. I made a decent haul that way.

Our trio was so terrible that Woods kept telling Dave, "That son of a bitch Freeman's got to go," and Dave kept saying, "If Bud goes, I go," so I stayed. Finally Dave got sick of our trio and left for another job, and the day he did Woods grabbed me by the collar and shouted, "You little bastard, if you're not out of here in five minutes I'll kill you!" Believe me, I got my things together and took off.

When I got home with all my money my father said, "Now son, where did you get all that?" I said, "Playing in the band and playing a slot machine." It took him a while to believe my story, but afterward he felt better about my future.

That same year Bill Grimm introduced us to another great musician. He called and said, "Listen, there's a wonderful black piano player who has just come to Chicago from Pittsburgh. I don't know his name, but I heard about him and he's going to play at a place called the Elite Gardens." He was talking about Earl Hines.

Well, we went down there and were just knocked out. I had never heard anybody play like him. Frank Teschemacher and Dave Tough and I started listening to him regularly; we used to stand behind his upright piano. He was just fantastic. He had a beat like a horn player, and he played single notes—like a trumpet player—against a very strong bass.

I think Earl was the first one to play piano with that kind of drive. As a young kid I used to tell him how wonderful and unique his style was. He was very modest. "No," he'd say, "there are three or four piano players in New York that will scare you to death." He was talking about James P. Johnson, Fats Waller, Luckey Roberts, and Willie "The Lion" Smith. Later on when I really got into jazz and made a study of it, I discovered those piano players and realized how honest Earl was and how great those guys really were.

Naturally, during these years of intense listening I was playing, or trying to play, with the others. Our gang kept rehearsing together and playing at dances and parties. Some of the guys went off and got jobs on their own. Tesch and I weren't the closest of friends (I didn't think of him as a dear friend after hearing that he wanted to throw me out of our band), but he and I had a lot of things worked up. We were a sax team. From 1924 through 1927 we played a number of dates together, both with the Austin High Gang and with others. One of our first jobs in 1924 was a weekend gig with trumpeter Wingy Manone, who had a band at the Merry Gardens.

Tesch was not terribly happy; in fact, he was a very temperamental, unsmiling fellow. If you said something humorous or friendly to him, he'd take offense and say, "What do you mean?" He truly loved the music, though, there's no doubt about it. He idolized Bix, and I think he was the first white guy to try to play like Jimmie Noone, and he did a pretty good job of it.

After Tesch and I made our famous recordings in 1927 with the

McPartlands, Jim Lannigan, Joe Sullivan, and Gene Krupa, we drifted apart and I never saw much of him. But in 1925 we were hanging out, and one night we went to a club called Palmer Katie's Cascade Roof on the far North Side. Palmer Katie's was a hangout for jazz musicians. On this particular night we sat in with the band and were paid fifty cents each.

Eddie Condon's brother Pat was in the band and Eddie was in the audience listening and he was impressed with us. He was two years older than Tesch and I. In fact, he and Pat had played a banjo act in vaudeville for several years, and Eddie had been playing professionally since he was fifteen. He knew Bix and was a fan of black music. He was a wise-cracking guy and a promoter and we were fascinated with him. Mezz Mezzrow, a wild man if ever there was one, named him "Slick" because he was such a sharp dresser and a wiseacre. He always wore bow ties and clothes he couldn't afford.

Most of our crowd dressed sharply in those days. We got our style from the Prince of Wales, who later became Edward VIII. Our clothes were very British. We bought fine English suits made from Scottish wool for about $25. Ordinarily they sold for about $100, but we knew a place on Roosevelt Road that sold odd lots at bargain prices. For all we knew they might have been stolen. We got our shoes, the finest in the country, at another place that sold them cut-rate at $12–15. Drummer Zutty Singleton always broke up laughing when he saw our new shoes. He would say, "Those Chicago guys, they haven't got a dime but they wear $50 shoes."

That same year, in 1925, I met Bix Beiderbecke and Louis Armstrong. I met Bix first, through Harry Gale, a friend of Dave Tough's and a damn good drummer. I was nineteen when Harry took me to hear Bix, who had just left the Wolverines and was sitting in with Charlie Straight's band at the Rendezvous on the near North Side. It was a band that played for dancing and a floor show; all the big stars used to go there. As Harry and I entered the club I saw Bix with his cornet about fifty feet away. Our eyes seemed to meet. Here I was facing this great genius I so idolized. Harry knew him, so we went backstage after the last set and waited for the band to walk off. That night I had one of the great thrills of my life.

I told Bix how excited I was to meet him, that I had heard every record he had made. He sat down at the piano and started to play compositions by Debussy and Eastwood Lane, his favorite. Then he played some of his own. I rattled on, telling him how great I thought his compositions were, almost embarrassing him with my compliments. He said, "Look, if you think this is good, did you ever hear of Hoagy Carmichael?" I said, "No," and he said, "Wait till you hear him play. This is one of his tunes." And he played "Boneyard Shuffle." While he played he told me all about Hoagy. He practically raved about him. True, Hoagy was way ahead of his time and in my view became a great composer, but Bix was the real genius. In fact, Hoagy's tunes were taken from Bix's and Frank Trumbauer's phrases. (Trumbauer was a great friend of Bix's and a fine C-melody saxist with the Jean Goldkette band.)

If Bix had lived longer he would have become one of America's greatest composers. He had a love of the great composers of the day, such as Ravel, Holst, Schönberg, and Debussy. They were a big influence on Bix, and you can hear that influence in his playing of "In a Mist" and "Flashes" and "In the Dark." It was Bix who got Dave Tough and me into listening to them. They gave us a much better feeling for jazz. I think that what I've heard in the great symphonic composers I've been able to use in my playing, and to this very day I listen to all the symphonic music I can.

I saw Bix a few more times before he left town to join Goldkette. One night he said to Tesch and me, "I'm going to take you to hear the greatest singer in the world." We arranged to meet him at the club a few days later on his night off, and the three of us took a cab to the Paradise Gardens on Thirty-first Street.

Jimmie Noone had the band there, a quartet with George Mitchell on trumpet and Glover Compton on piano; I don't remember the drummer. That night was the first time I heard Jimmie Noone, who was a wonderful clarinet player. I had never heard anyone like him. He would become a powerful influence on Tesch. George Mitchell, who was a little hunchback, was known as "Little Mitch." I thought he was a great player with a pure sound, a pure style. He didn't play like Louis; he was his own man. I don't remember Compton's playing but I do remember he wore diamonds and was a hit with the ladies.

The quartet opened its first set at 12:30 and depending on the number of customers in the club might play till 5 or 7 A.M. Little Mitch and Jimmie both had jobs at the Dreamland Ballroom, where they played until midnight. By the time they arrived at the Paradise Gardens, Little Mitch would be so tired that he would fall asleep on the stand. When it was his turn to take a chorus, someone would nudge him and he would wake up, playing right on the beat. It was the damndest thing.

That first night, after the band began playing the introduction to Isham Jones's "I'll See You in My Dreams," a big black woman came striding out from backstage holding a fistful of dollars. As big as she was, she moved in a graceful kind of dance-walk. Her name was Bessie Smith. Almost at once I knew I was hearing a great voice. Her phrasing was exquisite, and she was making something religious out of a popular song. She sang twenty or thirty choruses, going from table to table. (In those days customers gave table singers money.) Bix had been drinking steadily since we met him at the Rendezvous (all the way down to the Paradise Gardens he had been swigging from a pint of gin), and by the time Bessie came to our table he was smashed and threw all of his money at her. Someone came over and picked up the money and gave it to her. She didn't skip a beat; she was all business. She had the most fantastic voice I was ever to hear, and from then on I bought every Bessie Smith record I could find.

I also got to know Louis in 1925, when he began playing at the Sunset Cafe at Thirty-fifth Street and Calumet Avenue. He was the soloist with the Carroll Dickerson band, which played a floor show. Dickerson was a violinist. His band was not sensational, but Louis was in it. Louis was the attraction; he drew people from all over. We used to go there once, twice, even three times a week, and everybody knew us: the waiters, the waitresses, the chorus, the band, the comedians. The comedians would later become quite famous—The Judge, Nicodemus, and the fellows who later went on to the "Amos and Andy" television series.

You could buy underworld booze at the Sunset, but some people brought their own liquor and put it under the table and were served setups. Most of the patrons were black. It was a nightclub that must have held about a hundred people, a square room with a low bandstand about a foot off the ground and doors off either side for the chorus girls to come through. Most people went there for the booze or a woman; we went there for the music. The Sunset had one of the best floor shows I've ever seen. People talk about the floor show at the Cotton Club in New York, which was considered a much classier place, but the Sunset had Louis

Armstrong. Show people who were doing a date in Chicago and had heard of Louis went down. I remember Ted Lewis, a cornball clarinetist and band leader, came down one night and stood in front of the bandstand. Louis always played with his eyes closed, and Lewis stood there telling him to open them. He didn't understand that Louis was concentrating.

A year after Earl Hines came to Chicago to play the Elite Gardens, Louis talked him into joining the Dickerson band at the Sunset Cafe. In fact, Tesch, Jimmy, and I told Louis about Earl. Earl was being talked about, word had spread fast, and perhaps Louis had already heard of him from others, I don't know, but shortly after we mentioned Earl to Louis, Earl joined the Dickerson band. Louis had left King Oliver in 1924 to go with Fletcher Henderson's band in New York. He didn't like New York, however, and came back to Chicago in 1925 to join Dickerson, who had a great drummer, Tubby Hall. Tesch and I were there for the opening. I'll never forget how happy Louis was because Earl was playing with him. Although Earl would probably never have admitted it, I think he was very much influenced by Louis. I could hear it all in his right hand. That punching, single-note, righthand style was the trumpet style, and that was the secret of Earl's powerful and beautiful playing.

Louis influenced the whole world, not only horn players but arrangers and composers, who stole ideas from his old records and performances. Of course, hundreds of musicians who were influenced by Louis's playing did not have his wonderful sense of rhythm, his wonderful beat, his powerful sense of meter and melodic line control. It was just incredible the way the man could play, and every trumpet player who could hit a high C commercialized on it and said nothing.

I don't think there will ever again be anything in the world like the Sunset. Things just happened spontaneously there, and you never knew what was going to happen next. It gave me the best musical education I ever had.

After the Sunset closed at 3 A.M. we would go across the street to the Apex Club. That is when its music started. The Apex was small, but it too had a floor show. The band was led by Jimmie Noone, one of the finest clarinet players in Chicago. He was from New Orleans. His quartet had Earl Hines and a drummer named Ollie Powers, who was a table singer. Ollie would get up from the drums and go from table to table singing in this wonderful voice. The fourth musician was King Oliver's old guitarist, Johnny St. Cyr. What a band!

A couple of times after the Apex closed, at about five or six o'clock, we went next door to a speakeasy called the Bookstore. It was called that because it had one book in the window. You walked through a small front room into the back, which had a tiny stage. There was a black band that played there, led by a woman trumpet player named Dolly Hutchinson. She was very much influenced by the wonderful beat of church singing and also by Louis, I think. We loved her. She was young—probably under twenty—and tall, very slender, with a very lovely loose walk, no affectation and no showmanship—which was probably her showmanship. She was very sweet. I haven't the faintest idea what became of her.

After the Sunset closed one morning I went with several of Louis's musicians to the Apex. Jimmie's band was on break and a light-skinned man whom I had never seen before was bent over the piano. I walked over to Jimmie, pointed at the man, and asked, "Who's that?" "Jelly Roll Morton," he said. Morton was one of my idols. Floyd O'Brien had a complete collection of his records, and the Austin High Gang would go over to Floyd's house and sit up all night playing them. Now here was Jelly Roll in the flesh and I was thrilled. I walked up behind him and stood listening. Suddenly he jerked around, looking quite frightened. "I'm sorry," I blurted out. At that he relaxed and smiled. "Oh, no," he said. "That's all right, young man."

I sat down to listen as he continued playing his wonderful compositions. He was a good musician, and he had created a new style of playing. He wasn't a ragtime musician, he was more of a swinger. The rhythms in his music were very much like the rhythms of the Caribbean islands. I found that out much later, after hearing the music of the island blacks and having thought about Jelly Roll's music over the years.

I loved the way he sang, or rather talked. I could tell he didn't think he had much of a voice. He played several pieces, and one had a refrain that went: "I thought I heard Buddy Bolden say, 'Funky butt, funky butt, take it away.'" He was talking about an idol of his, Buddy Bolden, the New Orleans cornetist who is credited with having put together the first Dixieland combination in New Orleans.

When he finished playing and Jimmie's group got back on the stand,

I joined Jelly Roll and three or four other musicians at a table. Jelly Roll was very elegant, very handsome and well dressed. He wore expensive jewelry; later I heard that he had a way with women. When Jimmie's band finished its last set Jelly Roll turned to me and asked, "Have you heard Dolly Hutchinson?" I told him I had, and he asked if I wanted to go with him to hear her that night. So there I was, at about 5 A.M., heading for the Bookstore with the great Jelly Roll Morton.

I ran into him occasionally after that, especially during the period when he was recording his own compositions for his excellent Red Hot Peppers sessions with Victor. Some of the musicians he used for those sessions included Little Mitch, Johnny St. Cyr, and Omer Simeon, an excellent clarinetist and alto saxist.

One fellow who sometimes accompanied us on our excursions to the South Side was a University of Chicago student named Knowles Robbins. Knowles was a most unusual person; he didn't bother behaving like other people and didn't care what others thought about it. He was about five years older than the rest of us, and I think it was he who inspired Dave Tough's interest in literature and painting. Dave had been playing for frat parties at the University of Chicago from the time he was fifteen and had probably met Knowles at one of them. Knowles came from a brilliant family; one of his relatives had co-authored a book called *The Knowles-Favard System of French*. Knowles knew the language intimately. In fact, he used to think in French; in the middle of his dreams he'd say, "Mon Dieu."

After one night and morning of listening to music on the South Side, Knowles, Dave, and I arrived at the University of Chicago at 7 A.M. and flopped at Knowles's frat house. Shortly after stretching out, Knowles got a call from the man who played the carillon at Rockefeller Chapel. The man was ill and asked Knowles if he would ring the bells for him that morning. Knowles, who was drunk, said yes and staggered over to the chapel, played "Yes, We Have No Bananas," and was promptly expelled from school. About two years later he returned to the university to become one of its best French teachers.

Knowles was an amateur musician. He and many other students at the University of Chicago liked our style of music, and several frat houses besides his used to hire us for dances. Students at Northwestern University liked the new music too. In fact, there was a group of guys at the University of Chicago and a group at Northwestern, each of which played its own style of jazz. They couldn't have made it as pros, but playing helped them get through school. Northwestern even had its own style of tenor playing, which was appropriately called "the Northwestern style." I heard half a dozen players who had that style, which was similar to what Lester Young later developed. It was a light sound. I think the first guy to become a professional success with that style was Jack Pettis, who played with the New Orleans Rhythm Kings and later with Ben Bernie, a big-band leader and comedian.

Arny and I were still living at home, and he often went with us on these all-night sessions. My mother, as I said, had died several years before, and my father let us have our own way because he knew the two of us were creative. We were not paying any rent. The neighbors kept badgering him, saying, "Why don't your sons go out and get jobs like other boys? Why do you let them run around?" Dad would say, "My sons are not like other boys. They're artists." Well, he had been hearing that for months and it must have finally gotten to him. One morning when Arny and I lay in bed—we had just gotten in from one of our all-night sessions—Dad came into the bedroom and shook us. I was rolled up under the covers and pretended to be asleep, but Arny pulled the covers from over his head. My father said, "You've had enough of this free and easy life. You're going to get jobs and from now on behave as normal young men!" Arny sat straight up and in stentorian tones proclaimed, "How dare you, sir, wake us before the weekend!" Dad sheepishly left the room and never mentioned the subject again.

I was so involved in listening to jazz that I can't tell you what life was like in those days. We did not live as other people did. Music was twenty-four hours a day. When we weren't performing we were listening. Whenever a new Bix or Louis record came out we would have a party. Some guy would serve wine and food at his parents' home and we would discuss the record, but not as critics would. We talked about phrases. We would sing a phrase and play it over and over. We were learning, but we were learning through feeling. No one was invited who did not feel it. This is what we did for years on end.

This is what I mean when I say we lived the music. I used to go to the black churches to hear the singing and to hear the most wonderful beat in music, the most inspired jazz I've ever heard. That is where jazz, I think, really came from—from the black churches and from black tap dancing. Unlike other kinds of dancing, tap dancing seemed to tell a story about life, and I was as thrilled by it as I was by jazz.

"I Don't Believe It"

By the summer of 1925 I was playing tenor sax. Just before I picked it up I studied clarinet with Duke Riehl, who was an excellent teacher—in fact I never found anything written that was as difficult as the exercises I played for him. After studying with Duke for six months I could read well and play passably.

I got my first job on tenor that summer up at Lost Lake, Wisconsin, with Dick McPartland, Dave North, Frank Teschemacher, and Dave Tough. Jimmy McPartland had gotten a job there the year before through a pianist named Fritz Nielson from the University of Chicago. When Jimmy left to join the Wolverines he recommended us to Nielson and that's how we got the job. It was a wonderful place, quite a ways up in northern Wisconsin, near Eagle River and Sayner. We lived in log cabins, drank bootleg whiskey, and dressed like lumberjacks. It was one of the greatest jobs ever.

I used to take my horn into the woods at Lost Lake and practice long tones. Now Tesch was always very competitive, and one day he heard me and ran into the dining room where the guys were finishing dinner and said, "I've got to get my clarinet! I just heard Bud. He's got a beautiful tone."

The next year I met a very curious alto player named Mezz Mezzrow. Mezz came from a wealthy family that owned a chain of Chicago drugstores, but he was a little different from his relatives. He lived in a small apartment in Rogers Park and wanted to be his own man. Teschemacher and I met him one night when we went out to hear a drummer in a Chinese restaurant on the North Side. In those days Chinese restaurants hired dance bands which played floor shows. There were many of them all over the country that were able to hire bands and pay very good salaries.

We went to this one to hear Don Carter, who was a drummer. It was through Carter that we met Mezz. Carter, by the way, was Gene Krupa's earliest influence. The idea of chewing gum and making all the facial expressions that Gene used came from Carter, who in those days was one of the best white drummers in Chicago. He never became known outside the city, which was a pity because he was so great.

Mezzrow had heard of Tesch and me and was very friendly. He really loved music and had some new records in his house that had just come from New York and he invited us over. When we got there he opened a closet and here were all these bottles of gin without any labels on them. I said, "My God, how do you get this liquor without labels?" He said, "I'm a bootlegger." He was incredible, a combination alto sax player and bootlegger.

We started listening to jazz records regularly with him. Mezzrow loved the music as we did, but I didn't feel that he had gotten into as much listening as we had because he loved Red Nichols. Now in the opinion of our group Red Nichols was a synthetic player. He was a clever musician and made a lot of records, but he was a very mechanical player. He copied every line he had ever learned in jazz from Bix. When I first met Bix I talked about that and asked him what he thought of Red Nichols; I knew what I thought of Nichols, but I wanted to know what he thought. Bix said, "Well, he's making a lot of money." That was a polite way of answering.

Despite his taste Mezzrow was a great help to many of us with his enthusiasm. He was also the first white man I ever knew to move to Harlem and marry a black woman and have a child by a black. I had to love that about him because we lived in a time when prejudice was unbelievable. Mezz was a very strong human being and knew things about the black people, their way of thinking and their music, that very few white people did.

By early 1926 the gang was getting into its stride. The year before Jimmy had gotten a telegram from New York asking him to replace Bix in the Wolverines. Jimmy took the slot, but the band didn't have much work and the original members kept dropping out. As they did Jimmy replaced them with members of our group. By the summer of 1926 most of the Austin High Gang were in the band. Husk O'Hare was our booking agent and we called ourselves Husk O'Hare's Wolverines. Jimmy led the group, which had Dave Tough, Tesch, Floyd O'Brien, Jim Lannigan, Dave North, Dick McPartland, and me. We had two jobs. The first was for about a month at a dime-a-dance ballroom in Des Moines, Iowa, where we played our regular numbers. In dime-a-dance ballrooms guys would pay a dime for a ticket which entitled them to a short dance with one of the girls who worked there. At this hall a dance was three minutes long with a minute intermission during which the patrons would buy tickets for the next dance.

After that engagement ended weeks went by without any bookings from O'Hare. We were going down to the union hall every Monday looking for club dates but there weren't any. Not only was I out of work but so was my brother, Arny. Then Mezzrow came up with an idea. According to Mezz I was going to be the next Rudolph Valentino, and the sooner we got to Hollywood to let the producers know that, the sooner we'd all be sitting in the catbird seat. It just so happened that Mezz had a Hupmobile which he hadn't bothered to make any payments on, and he was anxious to get out of town before the repo man caught up with him.

It was strange, but Mezzrow actually believed that I would become a star, become rich and support him and Arny. After he announced his grand idea to us, Arny and I packed in about one minute. We called Josh Billings, a boyhood friend of ours, and asked him if he wanted to go and he said yeah and was over in five minutes. I never believed that I would become a movie star; we were just crazy kids who would do anything at the drop of a hat. There was no purpose to the trip as far as Arny, Josh, and I were concerned; we just didn't give a goddamn. We had homes we could always come back to and we never thought things over very much.

Between the four of us we might have had about twenty dollars, which ran out by the time we got to Kansas City. There we found a small theatrical hotel owned by a woman who had a lot of sympathy for us. She said, "Look, if you fellows want to wash some windows I'll give you dinner and let you stay for the night." We spent the rest of the day washing windows.

The next morning when we went downstairs we found out that Mezz's Hupmobile had been impounded. There we were, stranded in Kansas City with no money and no means of getting out of town. The only things we had of value were my clarinet and my tenor and soprano saxes. I hocked them for $125 and with that money bought a beat-up Ford touring car. We would have made better time with bicycles; that car did nothing but break down.

Outside of Lyons, Kansas, we had to get six other people to help us push the car up a long hill to a gas station. About a half dozen farmers were sitting around there smoking corncob pipes. They were curious to know where we were from and where we planned to go. We told them and said we were having a rough time and hadn't eaten in several days. They said there was going to be a barn dance that night and that we could come and have some shredded wheat, corn, and milk. When we got there about thirty people were dancing and socializing. We entertained them with stories about the jazz musician's life in Chicago. Josh tinkled away on the piano, my brother played the drums, and I did a little dance. I've long forgotten what Mezzrow did.

With that nourishment in us we pushed on as far as Pueblo, Colorado. How we made it there in that Ford I'll never know. We ran into a fellow in Pueblo who liked musicians and he let us stay at his home for the night while he went off to see his lady friend. Well before morning he came back laughing. It seems that his lady friend had a husband and he had caught the two of them in bed. The husband went for his shotgun as the man dove out a window. The husband fired but missed, and our host came back laughing. Everybody carried guns in Pueblo. It was a cowboy town then, and for all I know it still is.

That did it for the trip as far as I was concerned. I'd had enough of Pueblo and whatever else awaited us on the road. Josh and I called our parents and got the money for three bus tickets home. We climbed aboard a bus and waved good-bye to Mezz.

When we got back I found that my father was not upset at all. He was a wonderful man. He had been telling everyone that his sons were out in Pueblo, Colorado, which was a big thing in our neighborhood. Dad sent my pawn ticket with a check to the pawnshop in Kansas City and in about ten days I got my instruments back. When Monday came around I went to the union hall to look at job postings, and Lord, there was Mezzrow! How he got back I never found out.

Husk O'Hare's Wolverines soon had a job at the ballroom at the White City Amusement Park on the South Side. We played there the rest of the summer. In December of 1926, just before or just after the Goldkette band broke up, Frank Trumbauer, Pee Wee Russell, and Bix got a job at a ballroom at a summer resort in Hudson Lake, Indiana. Trumbauer was leading this outfit, whose members all played with Goldkette. Bix and Pee Wee had come to hear our band at White City because they had heard so much about it. We, of course, were honored to have them there. Dave Tough was playing in our band and they absolutely flipped over us. They invited us to go to hear them at Hudson Lake. We left on a Saturday night and got there on Sunday morning. Bix and Pee Wee were rooming together in a lake cabin. When we got there we banged on their door and when nobody answered we walked in. There they were, completely passed out; they had been drinking pretty heavily. We shook Pee Wee and he just sort of woke up swinging; he thought somebody was attacking him. A few minutes later we were jamming, and since I hadn't brought my sax I grabbed some sticks and began knocking out a beat on the back of a chair.

We slept that morning and then went with them to their afternoon session at the ballroom. It was amazing how beautifully they played with their terrible hangovers. I suppose they had their little drinks sitting up on the bandstand, but there was one thing about Bix: he might have had a few drinks just to nurse his hangover but I do not recall ever seeing him play drunk. He played so magnificently all the time. Pee Wee was a very good musician, too, something a lot of people don't understand. He could play those difficult tenor parts in the Goldkette band. He was playing tenor that day and asked me to sit in, which I did. He played the instrument beautifully but I couldn't get a sound out of it. Probably no one but Pee Wee could. When the horn needed pads he didn't replace them, he just put rubber bands on the keys to bring them back into place.

After we left the White City ballroom all of us were hired by a commercial bandleader named Art Kassel who had a pretty good idea what kind of sound he wanted. He got a job in Detroit at the Greystone Ballroom, where the Goldkette band had been playing. We alternated with the Fletcher Henderson band. Our band, for what it was, was good. We were at the Greystone for ten or eleven days. I remember we used to go across the river to a place in Canada to drink that wonderful Canadian ale and eat spaghetti. That was our breakfast.

It was when we were at the Greystone that I heard the great Coleman Hawkins. I'm not sure that I was influenced by him; I doubt very much that you could hear any influence of Hawkins in my playing. But I was influenced by the idea that the tenor could be played with such powerful authority.

You must understand that we, the white tenor players, and even the black, were not soloists. I played what you might call an "accompanimental" kind of tenor. I would weave in and out between the cornet and clarinet and get out of the way of the trombone too. It was not until I heard Hawkins that I realized what a powerful solo instrument the tenor could be, and it was after hearing him that I became a soloist. I owe that to him.

Hawkins was a superb musician. I prefer the playing of Lester Young and Ben Webster but I do think that Hawkins, although he did not play with their taste, was a better musician. He had a degree in music and played cello and piano too. He was kind of a loner, and I didn't hang out with him then, though he was very nice to me. I got to know more of him later on in New York, when I went there to join Ben Pollack's band. I even made an album with him and we played an original tune of mine for which he wrote out a little chart.

As long as I was in Detroit I hung out a lot with Fletcher Henderson and Joe Smith, the great, beautiful trumpet player who made those early records with Bessie Smith and Ethel Waters. Fletcher and Joe took me to the black late-hour spots to hear wonderful musicians, and we were always treated beautifully. I was very flattered that a world-renowned bandleader would bother at all with a young kid, and a white kid at that, and take him to all those places. But he got a big kick out of it.

I was twenty years old then and Rex Stewart, a fine trumpeter in Fletcher's band, was about the same age. He knew that I knew Louis Armstrong. Louis was around Chicago then, and I was going back there since the Kassel band had broken up. Rex was going back to New York with Fletcher to play the Roseland Ballroom so he gave me a note to give to Louis. Now bear in mind that it wasn't in an envelope, it was just a piece of folded paper on which Rex had written a letter to Louis in longhand. I couldn't resist reading it before I gave it to him. "Dear Rubber Lips: You are my idol. God bless you and keep on blowin'. Your boy, Rex." I'll never forget that note because Rex had never met Louis, he just idolized him so.

Back in Chicago I got a job working in a Chinese restaurant; in fact, Mezzrow got me the job. He went to this commercial bandleader, a violinist by the name of Milt Teller, who was getting a band together. I think I made eighty-eight dollars a week, which was a tremendous amount of money when you think of the year because there were no taxes then.

The next job I got in 1927 was with a bandleader named Herb Carlin. We played a floor show for dancing in a place on the North Side called the Hollywood Barn. During that time Paul Whiteman came to town to play at the Chicago Theater. He had Bix, Frank Trumbauer, and the Dorsey brothers. We used to go in the afternoons to see the show, which was fantastic.

While he was with Whiteman at the Chicago Theater Beiderbecke found a piano in a sawdust floor cellar at 222 North State, a block away from the theater. They were doing maybe five shows a day at the theater with Whiteman. Bix would get some gin and sit and play in this cellar between shows. Musicians soon found out about it and started coming down in the evenings for jam sessions. When the public heard about it they started coming too. I remember that Red McKenzie, who had the Mound City Blue Blowers, was in town and we met him down there and that's how he and Eddie Condon got together.

McKenzie was a former jockey turned "jazz" musician and promoter who came to town with his band in 1927. That band started off in St. Louis with McKenzie playing comb with tissue paper, Dick Slevin playing kazoo, and Jack Bland playing banjo. Red was Condon's opposite number, an unpolished character, sort of hard-boiled. He was so afraid of appearing effeminate that he talked out of the side of his mouth and dressed like a truck driver trying to slick up for a night on the town. After he met Condon at 222 North State McKenzie started hanging around with the Austin High Gang and eventually added Dick McPartland to the Mound City Blue Blowers.

Now I was playing at the Hollywood Barn until about three or four in the morning. One night Eddie called me at the club and said, "Bud, get your horn and come down, they're going to have a big jam session at 222 North State tonight when the Whiteman band gets through. We'll be there very late. Come at four o'clock, it doesn't make any difference." When I got there the place was so jammed I could hardly make it down the stairs. Tommy Dorsey, Jimmy Dorsey, Benny Goodman, and Ben Pollack were there. I don't know if Whiteman came, but many of the guys in his band were there. Condon was there and so were Teschemacher and Bix. Pollack heard me play tenor for the first time and Bix immediately complimented me on it. Not long after that we made our first recording for OKeh Records.

It was Red who was responsible for getting us that date. He had a lot of nerve. He went up to OKeh Records and insulted one of the producers and got us a recording session. It was Condon's date, but McKenzie arranged it. The group was called the Condon-McKenzie Chicagoans, with Eddie on banjo, Joe Sullivan on piano, Jim Lannigan on bass, Jimmy McPartland on cornet, me on tenor, Teschemacher on clarinet, and Gene Krupa on drums. Dave Tough, our regular drummer, was in Europe, and the closest thing we could find to Dave was Gene. He was eighteen years old.

Critics later claimed that we developed the so-called Chicago style, but the credit for that really belongs to King Oliver and Louis. What we did was to popularize the tenor saxophone in jazz bands. Not many bands had them in those days. The Wolverines did, but the average jazz band had a trombone instead.

By the time we recorded I had developed a very strange tenor style; it was like no one else's. That I would have something so different was only natural because I had absorbed so many different influences. Bix's and Louis's were probably the biggest. Black church singing and black tap dancing made powerful impressions on me, too, but so did King Oliver, Earl Hines, Dave Tough, Bessie Smith, Ethel Waters, James P. Johnson, and Willie "The Lion" Smith. The modern French composers were great influences harmonically. Because of all of them I knew that mine was not a style that was going to become old-fashioned and belong to a particular era.

By 1927 I had absorbed all of these influences except the Harlem pianists. I had come into my own voice. Of course, in 1927 I knew nothing about melodic line; it takes a lifetime to learn how to play a melody. It takes musical validity. As regards the development of my style, I don't recall ever saying, "I want to be different. I don't want to play like anybody else." My style was just the result of so much listening. I don't think I was conscious of its unique character until people came to me and said, "How does it happen you don't sound like anybody else?"

At any rate, on the strength of my solos on "Nobody's Sweetheart," "Liza," and "China Boy" for the OKeh date, I got an offer to go with Ben Pollack's band.

CHAPTER THREE

"Swingin' without Mezz"

Don Redman, who arranged and played saxophone with the Fletcher Henderson band, was in Chicago when I got the offer. I ran into him in January 1928, the day before I was to join Pollack in New York. Don said, "Bud, you're not going to like it in New York." I said, "Why do you say that?" and he said, "They don't swing there." "What do you mean?" I asked. "You mean nobody swings?" He said, "Nobody swings there. It's not like Chicago. Chicago is *it* for swing. Whenever we go out to Chicago we know we're gonna have to play better. This is where people hear and know and feel music."

I don't think geography has anything to do with music, but it's true that Chicago was a place that did swing. It was the center of jazz in those days, not New York. Bear in mind that New Orleans got the publicity but it never supported jazz. The great musicians had to leave there to make a living. Some went to New York, but most went to Chicago, which became the mecca, the center of jazz. There's no doubt about it. The Kansas City musicians played with the same beat as the Chicago players because they were so close to Chicago that they could go there to hear Louis and King Oliver. The best black players in the world were playing in Chicago at that time, with the exception of the great pianists, who were all around Harlem in New York.

I remember that in the beginning I didn't really like New York. The Pollack band was playing at the Little Club, a posh night spot. We had Jimmy McPartland on cornet, Al Davis on trumpet, Benny Goodman on clarinet, Benny's brother Harry on bass, Dick Morgan on guitar, me on tenor, Gil Rodin on alto, Pollack on drums, Glenn Miller on trombone, and Vic Breidis on piano. We could play anything written, but we were not commercial. We were wild kids and here we were playing a floor show for a very high-class act in a club that catered to famous journalists and theater people such as the Barrymores.

Jimmy McPartland and I shared a room at the Mayflower Hotel. It was quite elegant but we could afford to stay there because between us we were making about $1,000 a week. We never had a bank account; we just threw all of our money into a drawer. If I took out $100 I would say, "Hey, Jimmy, I took out a hundred bucks today," and he would go over and take out a hundred too. We never kept records.

We just seemed to live in this crazy world and thought we would always be very successful. After all, we were suddenly on top of the music business after having had it tough in Chicago for so many years, working all night in dumps. Most of Pollack's musicians had played in Chicago and knew what it was like to work in sawdust places. It had not depressed us, however, because we had been doing what we wanted, playing a kind of music we loved and wanted to develop.

Dick Morgan was as wild as Jimmy and me, or anyone else in the band for that matter. We called him "Icky" because he used to make a strange face like an ichthyosaur. In those days there was a film called The Lost World and in it this monstrous ichthyosaur sticks its big face into a skyscraper window. Dick used to make a face like that dinosaur whenever he got into one of his crazy moods or when he was drinking. He would make that face and talk as you might imagine the dinosaur would talk. He also wrote something he called "Icky's Blues," with lyrics that went, "Eek ecky pabby wacky dacky icky bull." It used to bowl me over.

Now all the clubs in those days had floor shows, and we were playing serious music for one that featured a very elegant dance team. One of their numbers was a waltz from The Student Prince. The man on the team dressed in the uniform of the student prince and the girl, who incidentally was the Waterman ink heiress and quite beautiful, wore gorgeous gowns. One night Icky and Harry Goodman got drunk. Harry, who was kind of fat, put on this trim guy's uniform and Icky put on one of the girl's lovely gowns and we played the show's beautiful music. They got down on the floor and rolled around and the customers broke up laughing.

On Sunday nights the club had a theatrical night and a lot of

Ziegfeld Follies girls and musicians would come in and get very drunk. The musicians would sit in with us and we would have a jam session. Jimmy Dorsey and Fud Livingston, a tenor saxist and clarinetist, used to come down and parody Ted Lewis, trying to see who could play the corniest. One night they were playing for Icky, Jimmy McPartland, and me. The three of us had a regular singing trio. We would get out on the floor and go from table to table and sing while Vic Breidis played for us. This night Jimmy Dorsey and Fud were playing, too, and they knocked over Vic's little upright piano and the boss practically threw us out of the place. We had not been there three months. We were damned good and we had a ball, but we were kids who were not serious about our careers. After being fired we did a tour of one-nighters until we hit a long period in which we didn't do anything. I went home to see Arny and some friends, then in June I got word from Pollack that we had a month-long job in Atlantic City and I left to rejoin the band.

Near the end of July I got a call from a banjo player named George Carhart, sort of a New York City society guy who wore a monocle. He was putting together a band to play on the *Ile de France* on her first voyage out of New York and he asked me to join him. I accepted because I wanted to see Dave Tough, who was still living in Paris. In a way, I had been on top of the music business with Pollack; certainly, he had the best band of its kind in America. It was a great thrill to sit next to an artist like Benny Goodman every night, but I left. The voyage turned out to be practically a free trip because I only played a few sets. Ted Lewis also had a band on the ship, and he had George Brunis with him. Brunis had been with the New Orleans Rhythm Kings and played an old-time New Orleans tailgate style. He wanted to impress us and tried to direct us once, but the poor fellow only looked ridiculous; he didn't know what he was doing.

It took six days to reach Le Havre, France. I went straight to Place Pigalle in Paris, to an Argentinian restaurant called L'Abbey, where Dave was playing in a band led by Danny Polo. Danny was a fine clarinet and saxophone player who had played with the Goldkette band. He had been to Europe before and had gotten an offer to go to Germany and had ended up in France. Dave had gone with him. At L'Abbey they were playing for a floor show and dancing. The Prince of Wales, later Edward VIII, used to go there on weekends with one of the Dolly sisters, give Dave a big tip, and sit in and play the drums. I sat in with Danny's band one night, too, and he and Dave wanted me to stay on, but I didn't want that kind of work. I wanted to remain a jazz soloist, so I returned to Chicago.

As soon as I hit town I went right to OKeh Records, where I had made my first recording in 1927. I walked right up to the producer and told him, "I'd like to do a record," and he said, "Fine." I brought in some Chicago guys, including Johnny Mendel, a very good trumpet player; Dave North, the Austin High pianist who now owned a printing business and just played as a hobby; and Bud Jacobson, a little-known but fine clarinetist. I also used Herman Foster on banjo and John Mueller on bass, along with Floyd O'Brien, Gene Krupa, and Jim Lannigan.

We did two sides, "Can't Help Lovin' Dat Man" and "Craze-O-logy." "Craze-O-logy," the side that's gotten more publicity, was named at the studio. I have had so many experiences at recording sessions where the recording engineer would say, "What's the name of this?" and I would say, "God, I don't know." A few times I have actually taken the title from him. For instance, there was a tune I recorded called "That D-Minor Thing." After we cut the record the engineer said, "Hey, can we take that D-minor thing? By the way, what's the title of it?" and I said, "You just mentioned it." We got titles that way.

"Craze-O-logy" got its name because while I was at the studio I remembered a tune of Trumbauer's called "Trombology." I liked the "-ology" part so I said, "Well, 'Craze-O-logy' might be a good title." I felt it sort of described the life I was living. I had not had a long-term job with any band since I began playing professionally, and I wouldn't until I joined Roger Wolfe Kahn in 1933. Until that year I went from one job to another, working in dime-a-dance joints and theater pits, in gangster-owned clubs and speakeasies. I even spent one night in a theater orchestra. During those years I kept going back and forth between Chicago and New York. When I was gone I always missed Chicago and still had a home there. My father never asked me for any rent and I could come and go as I liked. I would stay in New York for a few months and then return to Chicago. I was not to leave my home for good until 1933. I couldn't make up my mind what I wanted to do.

Now in 1928 I was back in Chicago and got a job with Zez Confrey playing in the Opera Club, another posh night spot. Zez, who wrote "Kitten on the Keys," was a marvelous pianist. He could not play jazz himself but he loved guys who could. He came to work every night with a chauffeur and a Rolls Royce. He was a super guy, and when very pompous people would come up and request tunes he would say, "I'm sorry, we don't play that." One night some guy made a remark and Zez said, "All right fellows, let's go," and we got up and walked off the bandstand.

So that job didn't last very long. The good jobs never did. I returned to New York and the week I got back Larry Binion, who took my place in the Pollack band, became ill. The band was playing in a Broadway show called *Hello Daddy* and doubling at the Park Central Hotel. I worked with them for a week. In the show I had a jazz solo of about six improvised choruses. Sitting behind me was a very fine musician who had been with a Russian opera company. He was a French horn player, and every night he'd look at me very quizzically because, although he knew composition, he'd never heard anyone improvise. One night he tapped me on the shoulder and said, "Hey, young man, someday dot's gonna be something vut you're doing." He knew.

In 1929 I lost all interest in playing music for money. I had just come to know Harlem and its wonderful way of life. Harlem was the home of the greatest, most creative jazz pianists the world will ever know. Willie "The Lion" Smith was one of them. Willie played in an after-hours club, a rendezvous for dancers, singers, actors, and musicians. There was constant chatter about a new play or a new piece of music or a new dance. Willie never appeared to be working; rather, he seemed more like a king holding court. I sat watching and listening to him for hours on end. What I felt for his music I could never put into words, but he knew how I felt and we became good friends. One night he told me that a great soprano saxophone player had just come back from France, where he had been imprisoned for many months for shooting a man. He had called Willie and was coming to the club to sit in. His name was Sidney Bechet. In my view he was the first great jazz soprano sax player. I'd never heard anyone like him before. He was very kind to me and invited me to play duets with him in his flat.

He had opened a small tailor shop there until he could again make a living playing music. As I mentioned earlier, I was not interested in playing music for money; and, of course, I looked like a beggar. One day Bechet looked me over and said, "Boy, how do you expect to make any kind of living looking like that? Take those pants off and let me press them for you." I've kept them pressed ever since.

Oftentimes when I was in New York I would play for dances at Ivy League schools. This was long before jazz concerts. In fact, the first jazz concert I played was at the Yale Club for Yale graduates in 1929. John Hammond, a record producer and a lover of jazz music who did a great deal to help Benny Goodman and many of the black players, was a graduate of Yale and he got us the job. I said to Benny, "What the hell is this?" and he said, "This is a concert." It was probably the first jazz concert ever.

What a contrast between the Ivy League schools and the Chicago gangster-owned clubs! I didn't particularly like playing those clubs, but there were few places not owned by gangsters where we could play the way we wanted. I remember the time I got a call from a man who said, "Would you come over and look at my place? I'd like you to put a band in here." I went over and there were all these underworld characters in black coats with collars turned up and guns on both hips. I was a little frightened and said to the boss, "I don't think I want to work here. You see, I want to finish my education and I would like to live long enough to do so." He put an arm around me and said, "Buddy, nobody in this here joint will hurt you unless he's paid for it." Well, I took the job but between sets I sat in a booth with a book. One night as I was reading Shakespeare's sonnets, the boss came over and said, "Read some of that." I did and he said, "Holy gee! You understand that and you're only makin' thirty-seven dollars a week and tips?" He was so impressed that he gave me a raise.

There were some good-paying jobs on the North Side but they didn't last as long as the South Side jobs did. Some South Side players, such as Jimmie Noone, stayed with jobs that lasted years; we whites counted the length of ours by weeks, sometimes days. The upshot was that we often had to piece odd jobs together to make ends meet. Once I worked about three weeks in a little dime-a-dance place in the Loop. Between sets one night I looked at the drummer and saw he was carrying a gun. I said, "Why are you carrying that?" and he said, "Jeez, Freeman, I can't make no money playing jazz."

I thought I had gotten my big break in 1930 when Floyd O'Brien and I received a telegram from Mezzrow asking us to come to New York. Mezz said he was going to organize the first black-white band. Now this happened long before John Hammond gave the idea to Benny Goodman. We went to New York and rehearsed. Alex Hill, the pianist, wrote a lot of the arrangements. We did a couple of club dates and then we got a job for a very short period. The band was too far ahead of its time. People weren't ready for it.

Poor Mezzrow, he was a very good friend and a great help to me, very encouraging, but he did not have the talent to run a band and he could not play the parts. I remember Alex was so broken-hearted. He told me, "My heart, my soul is in this band." Everything he wrote was a gamble for him; he wasn't paid very much to do these things. He wrote beautiful arrangements and Benny Carter brought over others, but the first saxophone parts were vastly difficult things and Mezzrow couldn't play them. One night after our first rehearsal Alex was drinking and suddenly he said, "Shit, Bud." He was crying. He said, "Mezz can't read." Alex's poor heart was broken. The fable all ended when we couldn't get any work. I started to record and play with other bands and got away from Mezzrow. I never went back to Chicago; I never went back home again. I stayed in New York and went from one band to another.

Work was sporadic in New York and the jobs didn't last too long. I took what I could. Recording sessions helped, and I did a lot of them in those days, usually for thirty dollars a session. Still, we were forced to take almost any job that came along. In 1930 I got a call from Jimmy Dorsey, who said, "Look, there's a theater opening in Jamaica this week and I'd like you to go over there and substitute for me for just one day. It's going to be a stage orchestra which will play an overture and there'll be a stage show. You're to play second clarinet. The program's going to be Chopin." I said, "Wait a minute, Jimmy, I can't play Chopin. I'm a jazz saxophonist." He said, "I know, but I've heard you play a little clarinet and you can handle the second clarinet part."

I did work on a lot of things with Jimmy, and in those days everybody doubled. The man who played tenor would double on the clarinet. So Jimmy talked me into doing it, and when I arrived at the theater I went directly to the first clarinet player and said, "Look, I can't play Chopin. I'm a jazz tenor saxophone player." He said, "Bud, I've got all of your records. I'll make a deal with you. Teach me how to play some jazz phrases and I'll help you do this thing." And this was the deal. I was not to make a sound; nothing was to come out of my clarinet. This man would cover me on the second clarinet parts and also play his first clarinet parts. "The conductor is drunk," he told me. "He won't know the difference."

When the stage rose and we went into Chopin I held the clarinet very properly with the bell on one knee and moved my fingers and swayed back and forth with the conductor, who was looking right at me. Now bear in mind that not a sound was coming out of my clarinet, yet he looked right at me and shushed me as though I were playing too loudly. I got ninety dollars for that. The next day when Jimmy called me to ask how it went I said, "Jimmy, call me for anything. Call me for the symphony. I know how to do it now."

During that year, 1930, I recorded three sessions with Hoagy Carmichael, who had come to New York the year before with a degree in law from Indiana and a stack of tunes he wanted to record. Hoagy got a contract from Victor Records, and Bix, who was helping him get the musicians, highly recommended me. At the first session we had Tommy Dorsey on trombone, Jimmy Dorsey and Benny Goodman on clarinet, Bubber Miley on trumpet, Bix on cornet, Joe Venuti on violin, Harry Goodman on bass, Gene Krupa on drums, Irving Brodsky on piano, and me.

We did a recording of "Stardust." "Stardust," of course, became a classic and Hoagy eventually must have become a millionaire through it. But we played it at the wrong tempo. Everybody in the band said, "Get rid of that stupid tune," and we threw it out. Six months or a year later, Isham Jones, the famous dance band leader, recorded it as a ballad and it became a tremendous hit and there wasn't a band in that era that didn't play it.

In those days, in order to please publishers you played a lot of terrible songs, and we had one called "Barnacle Bill the Sailor." The A&R man had probably said, "Hoagy, you've gotta have some tunes that are gonna sell." This one was about a drunken sailor. It's a stupid song; it sounded like a march but Bix played magnificently on it. I had a few bars; everybody had something to do on it. They asked Joe Venuti, because he had a gruff voice, to say at the end, "Barnacle Bill the shailor." He was supposed to be the drunken sailor. If you listen very closely you can hear him say, "Barnacle Bill the shit ass." The people at Victor didn't pick up on that; the musicians were the first people to find out.

We did about eight sides of Hoagy's things and then we did some things under Bix's name. On the strength of that album, I think, Hoagy began to catch on. After those sessions we soon found ourselves rehearsing a band to go to Europe. We had Bix on cornet; he was to lead the group. We also had Tommy Dorsey on trombone, Jimmy Dorsey on clarinet, me on tenor, Joe Sullivan on piano, Gene Krupa on drums, Dick McDonough on guitar, and Adrian Rollini on bass saxophone. We were rehearsing at the Roseland Ballroom in New York to do a ten-week tour of Europe when Bix became ill. He was sent back to Davenport, Iowa, his hometown, where he died a year later. What a tour that would have been, because we were famous there. We were not known in America, except to music people around New York, where we did a lot of recording.

Bix died in 1931. He had taken two or three alcoholic cures, and they can really knock everything out of you. He wasn't terribly strong or healthy after all the years of beating his body the way he did, but he was, I thought, in wonderful shape on those sessions. I spent a lot of time with him then and I do not recall that he was doing any drinking. Many people think that all their great jazz idols were addicts and drunks. But those jazz musicians who became drunks and addicts, had they not been musicians, still would have been drunks and addicts. The music didn't drive them to it. In fact, the music was the one thing that should have taken them away from it because you have to be sober to play well. Beiderbecke was an alcoholic, but he could not have played as beautifully as he did if he had been smashed out of his skull on a session. No one can play that beautifully and be drunk. Bix did his drinking after playing hours.

Two years after Bix died I wrote the wildest and the best known of my compositions, "The Eel." The title perfectly expresses the writhing, convoluted phrases of the composition, which in turn epitomizes the feeling I had for wild playing. "The Eel" evolved, in fact, from a phrase I first played in 1931 in Dowagiac, Michigan. I was on a date with Dick McPartland. I played a phrase that began in B-flat and modulated into the E-flat blues. Dick said, "That's wonderful, that's great. Do it again." I said, "I don't know if I can play it again." He broke up laughing and fell out of his chair. He said, "Why don't you make a composition out of that?" And that's how I got the idea for "The Eel."

I experimented with that phrase for two or three months, and by 1933 I had worked it into a composition and recorded it on an Eddie Condon date. Besides Eddie and me there was Alex Hill on piano, Pee Wee Russell on clarinet, Max Kaminsky on trumpet, Artie Bernstein on bass, Floyd O'Brien on trombone, and Sid Catlett on drums. A month later, with Joe Sullivan replacing Alex Hill, we rerecorded it. Then in 1939 I made yet another recording of "The Eel," this time with Danny Alvin on drums, Dave Bowman on piano, Eddie Condon on guitar, Clyde Newcomb on bass, Pee Wee Russell on clarinet, Brad Gowans on trombone, and Max Kaminsky on trumpet. That tune has been remembered, no doubt about it. I've been getting royalty checks on it ever since the Condon date, which makes me wish I had written another fifty tunes like it.

"The Time Is Right"

In 1933, the year I recorded "The Eel," I got an offer to go with Roger Wolfe Kahn. His band had some great players, including trombonist Abe Lincoln, saxist Toots Mondello, drummer Stan King, and the wonderful pianist and composer Fidgy McGrath. We had some fine arrangers, too, men who later went on to Hollywood and wrote for films. But as good as that band was, some of our jobs didn't last very long. As soon as some of the club owners heard that Roger was the son of the famous financier Otto Kahn, they would ask him to buy into the place. Since Roger didn't want to own any nightclubs or restaurants, he would say no and they would say they couldn't afford him anymore and let us go. This happened two or three times.

At one point we played at the Sun and Surf Club in Atlantic Beach, on Long Island, which was a rendezvous for the Dutch Schultz mob. We had several people in the floor show who would later become famous: Marge and Gower Champion, who at that time were dancers; Martha Raye, one of the band's singers; and the Ritz Brothers, a comedy team. One night after the show Martha did an imitation of the Ritz Brothers and broke everybody up. That's when some agent got the idea of making a comedienne out of her. She was a simple, very nice gal; her whole life was music. All of us, including Martha, would go out on the beach in the daytime and swim and play softball with the Dutch Schultz mob. Everybody loved her.

Toots Mondello and I left Roger when we got an offer to go with Joe Haymes. We stayed with his band for eighteen months. As regards big bands, Haymes had one of the finest. He had Pee Wee Erwin and Johnny Mince playing clarinet and sax, and Dan D'Andrea, an arranger and baritone player. During my last days with Haymes I was in bed with the flu, and on the night I came back Mondello said we'd all been asked to go with Ray Noble, the fine English bandleader, arranger, and composer. We accepted. Interestingly, there was a labor law condition that existed whereby an American band could not get into England and an English band could not get into the United States. But the Rockefellers, I think, were subsidizing Noble and he was brought in, along with his manager and drummer, Bill Harty.

In its time it was a pretty super band, and Ray himself was a beautifully educated, elegant man. When he first came to the United States we rehearsed and did a few recordings and club dates and had a radio show, the "Coty Perfume Hour." Because Ray spoke with an upper-crust British accent the men couldn't understand him when he spoke from the control room during rehearsals. He'd say, "Fellows, take the lahst eight bahs and there to the 'dalsegnah,' then to the tahp, then to the codah," and the guys would come over and say, "What the fuck did he say?" I was the interpreter because I was an Anglophile and had seen a lot of British plays.

After a few months of jobbing around we went into the Rainbow Room in Rockefeller Plaza. While we were there Ray got a call from a millionaire who was throwing a debutante party for his daughter in a very posh townhouse in New York. We worked the Rainbow Room until three in the morning and started the party at four. We were to play for an hour, probably for an astronomical fee. We went over to the townhouse and were met at the front door by the English butler, who waved us around to the kitchen. Ray said, "Out of the way," and we went in the front. Musicians in those days always had to go in through the kitchen, but we walked into the drawing room and sat there a few minutes before the debutante came and said, "Mr. Noble, aren't you going to play? We hired you." Ray said, "I believe the gentlemen would like some champagne first." No one had ever heard of musicians being so independent.

She didn't want to displease him so she sent downstairs for some champagne, and we sat there for about forty-five minutes before she came back and once more asked if we would play. Ray graciously assented, and we played for about an hour. Everybody loved the band

and came to Ray and said, "Would you play another hour?" He said, "Fellows, do you wish to play anymore?" The fellows said, "Ray, we are very tired." "Sorry, the chaps don't want to play anymore." They just didn't give a damn about the money. He was a big thing; he became a very big favorite.

Claude Thornhill was in the band then, a brilliant pianist and arranger. Claude and Ray didn't seem to get on too well. I don't know what the cause of the friction was, but Ray could have been holding Claude down because Claude did make some fantastic arrangements. I think there was some musical competitiveness there. Although Ray was a brilliant musician, I think Claude might have been a better one, and Ray sort of hid him behind the scenes.

Claude decided he would have no more of it. He was a very bright man but he also was a knocked-out kind of guy. One night the band had finished playing for the evening when Nelson Rockefeller came up with a party. The dressing rooms were one flight below the club. All of a sudden the band got word to go back up because Rockefeller was there with a private party and they wanted to hear music. The story goes that everyone went back upstairs. Thornhill was the last to go up, and for some reason he just went up wearing his shorts and tuxedo top. He played the whole hour in his shorts. He was wild.

The Rainbow Room had a revolving floor in front of the band. Ray would get up wearing white tie and tails and sit down at the piano on the revolving floor. We would go into a medley and Ray would play and talk to the people at the tables as he was being moved about. When he got about halfway around the circle he would be a half-block away from us. Claude would then change keys on him. Ray would be playing "The Very Thought of You," say in E-flat, and Claude would change it to F and Ray would be stuck out there. When a half hour later the piano, moving circularly, got back to the bandstand Ray would be furious, and he would say, "For God's sake fellows, I am playing 'The Very Thought of You' in E-flat. What the hell are you playing?"

There were two flights of stairs leading to a backdrop stage behind the band. Since Claude was building up in his mind the idea of leaving, and since he didn't want to do anything as dull as give two weeks' notice, he got very drunk one night and gathered up all of the very light plastic cases in which we put our arrangements. He got a piece of string and wrapped the cases around himself so they looked like a kind of a cape and staggered up the two flights of stairs to the top of the stage. The light man must have thought an act was going on, because he put a spot on him. Thornhill had this strawlike red hair that fell down over his face. That night he looked like Mr. Hyde when Mr. Hyde wasn't feeling too well. He put his hands over his head like Dracula, looked out at the people and said, "Ladies and gentlemen, I'm going to leave now and I doubt very much that I will ever be back." And that was the last time we saw him. For about a half hour there was no piano playing and Ray came down sort of upset and said, "For God's sake, where's Claude?"

I was with Ray for eighteen months and we became pretty good friends, but he did fire me because I wasn't doing things he wanted me to do. I was probably being a little wild and playing a lot of crazy things. One of the other saxophone players and I didn't get on too well, and he went to Ray and said, "Either Bud Freeman leaves or I leave." Glenn Miller told me this story. I don't know how true it is, but Ray did fire me.

After I left I did a short stint with Paul Whiteman on a program for the Woodbury soap people. Then I got an offer in 1936 to go with Tommy Dorsey. Although I was never really happy working with a big band, I came close to it with Tommy. The happiest I have ever been is when I've been playing with a combo, because combos allow me the freedom to play what I want. Big bands do not allow musicians that freedom. When you play in a big band you go into an arrangement, jump up and play eight or sixteen bars, and that's it. Only in the Dorsey band was I given all the freedom I wanted. I had a solo on just about every Dorsey chart. When we got into theaters, where we played five, six, maybe seven or eight shows a day, Tommy would put me out in front of the band for fifteen minutes and I'd play chorus after chorus. Tommy was very good to me, and in that way I was happy, but I hated the life because we lived in broken-down cars or in the little bus we had. We didn't fly and we rarely took trains; they were too expensive. The band didn't start to make money until Tommy's first hit record, "Marie."

There's an interesting story about how we got that song. We played in a little theater in Philadelphia called Nixon's Grand Theater. It had a black stage show and a black band in the pit that had a wonderful little arrangement of "Marie." I loved that arrangement and I went to the bandleader and said, "Would you mind if we made up an arrangement of that for our own band?" He said, "Go ahead." I went to Paul Weston and Axel Stordahl, Tommy's arrangers, and said, "I think we should do something with this fantastic song." They thought so too and did an arrangement of it. No one ever dreamed it was going to be a hit because this pit band had been doing it for years. Don Redman had done an arrangement of it too.

Let me explain something about this black theater. During this era it was bringing in all the well-known white bands, an unheard-of thing in those days, and the shows were selling out. Their black audiences really loved the white bands, and when I would get out in front to do my solos, the black people would get up in the aisles and dance. It was fantastic.

Anyway, after that engagement we went to Victor Records in New York. We were recording quite often in those days. We told Eli Oberstein, Victor's A&R man, that we wanted to do our arrangement of "Marie." He wasn't enthusiastic about it but we did it anyway and he finally issued it. That song made Tommy. It was his first hit record and the biggest one he ever had, no doubt about it. That was in 1937. From then on we started to make money. We worked the best hotels in the country, the best jobs. I must have recorded fifty sides with Tommy. We were so busy at one time that we used to have meetings to try to persuade Tommy to give us a week off. We had work, nothing but work. You can be very unhappy just working all the time.

Although Tommy could be a very hard man he was actually kind. He would do anything for you. It was just that he could not bear guys who couldn't play up to his standards. He was wonderful to Dave Tough, wonderful to me, wonderful to Pee Wee Erwin. Anybody whose playing he liked could get away with murder. He idolized Bunny Berigan, who was with us a short time. In fact, Bunny did some one-nighters with us and then made the original record of "Marie." He also had a powerful solo in "Song of India." Off the bandstand there was no kinder man than Tommy. He had done a lot of things for people, things we never heard about until we left the band. For example, even though he and Bunny had a fistfight one night, Tommy ended up financing Bunny's band.

It was too bad Bunny didn't know that he could have made a living as a soloist. He could have. Everybody, especially the young kids, loved him and his playing. He could have become a giant. But he was the last guy who should ever have had a band because he was too nice a person. You've got to be a strong, tough character to run one. Successful bandleaders don't give a goddamn what their musicians think of them, but Bunny loved everybody and needed that love in return. If a guy didn't like his playing or didn't like him personally, Bunny would be unhappy. And here all these young kids idolized him. Bunny's drinking was another handicap for him as a bandleader. You cannot drink and have a band. Tommy Dorsey said a very sage thing about Bunny. He said, "You know, anybody can have a band and make it. All you have to do is quit drinking." You can imagine how difficult that was for Tommy because he was a real drunk before he formed his band.

Even though Tommy was very unhappy about the way I played in the saxophone section, my solos pleased him so much that he was able to forget about my independent way of playing. When I say "independent" I mean I wasn't playing with the rest of the musicians. I was playing the arrangements but not well because I was always thinking about what I was going to do for my solo.

It wasn't difficult to get Tommy into a fight, but he never raised his hand to me. He would become angry and we'd shout back and forth and he would say, "You're fired!" At the end of the night he'd call my hotel and say, "Would you like to have a bite?" I'd join him and he'd say, "If I were you I could be the biggest thing in the world," and I would say, "Tommy, I am the biggest thing in the world," and I would go back and play the next night. At other times I'd quit and he'd say, "Come on back." As it turned out I was fired three times and quit four because I had to be one up on him.

One night at the Commodore Hotel he was so angry that he walked off the bandstand and the musicians couldn't get him to come back for three or four days. They said, "Bud, you call him up, you're close to him." I did and told him, "You're nothing but a big fucking baby." With that you could hear a pin drop. There was this dead silence. No one had ever talked to him that way. He was very wise in many ways and realized I was being his friend. No one else had called him; no one else had cared. He came back smiling like a big kid, as though nothing had happened. The day I left Tommy I went down to his dressing room to say good-bye. No one had done that before, because whenever anyone had left it had always ended in a big fight.

Tommy and his brother Jimmy fought all their lives like cats and dogs, but it was a love-hate relationship they probably didn't understand. After they broke up their band Jimmy formed another one and went to California where he had a contract with Bing Crosby. He did a radio show with Bing for a hell of a long time. When we played in San Antonio, Texas, for a month we went once a week to Dallas to do a radio show. We were substituting for Fred Waring. I was with Tommy then, and whenever he was going to do the broadcast he would say, "This has got to be good because the 'brother' is going to be listening." They had this competition all their lives.

Just before Tommy died he had a jazz concert on the "Jackie Gleason Show" and Jackie or Tommy hired several of us to appear on it. When Tommy died, Jackie turned his show over to Jimmy and we had a memorial to Tommy. There must have been some eighty or ninety musicians who had been with Tommy at one time or another, and they all showed up. Tommy had so many former sidemen that he must have broken an all-time record for personnel changes. If he didn't like a guy's playing, the guy was out. Many, many musicians quit too, of course. I remember Joe Venuti was at this tribute and we sat around a big round table and were telling stories about Tommy. Jimmy said, "Oh, how happy he'd be." That was the first sweet thing I ever heard Jimmy say about his brother. "How happy Tommy would be to be here now with us, because he loved these get-togethers." (Three years earlier, in 1953, Jimmy and Tommy had gotten back together with a beautiful band. Dick Cary and I wrote a half dozen things for them, one of which would have been a big hit, a tune called "The Time Is Right," but then Tommy died and that was the end of it.)

While I was with Tommy in 1937 Hoagy Carmichael became engaged and called me up to ask if I would bring an all-star group to the wedding reception. I brought Bunny Berigan, Dave Tough, Pee Wee Russell, Eddie Condon, and Joe Bushkin. Joe was our piano player but Hoagy sat in and played some numbers with us. A lot of Hoagy's well-known friends came, including Condé Nast and George Gershwin. I remember that Gershwin was a very unsmiling, egomaniacal man. That night I played about ten choruses of one of his tunes, and I don't think he ever forgave me. I'll never forget his expression; I was a little concerned. I could be mistaken, maybe he wasn't paying attention to me, but he did die not long after that.

The world thinks of Gershwin as a jazz composer but he wasn't. He was a damn good composer, but I don't really feel he understood a great deal about jazz, although he did listen to a lot of it. He heard Bix and used to go up to Harlem. You can hear the anticipated beat of the great blacks in Gershwin's works, but bear in mind that we all copied that beat. All of the composers who later became famous for their Broadway shows used to spend a lot of time in the twenties listening to the great Harlem piano players. They were probably playing that anticipated beat before Gershwin was born. But I think that Gershwin, if he had lived longer, would have become a very, very great composer. I think that "Rhapsody in Blue" is a work of art and, along with "Porgy and Bess," will live a long time.

Anyway, I left Tommy Dorsey in 1937 to go with Benny Goodman. I didn't really want to go with Benny, but Dave Tough and Jess Stacy were with him and they used to call up all the time, saying, "Come on, Bud. It's perfect. It's a real band, a real jazz band." They sold me a bill of goods and I made the greatest mistake of my life. What was I going to do in the Goodman band? He did all the playing, as well he should have. He was a great artist, but I was very unhappy there.

Just a few years earlier Benny had been struggling on the road and writing to people at NBC, looking into the idea of breaking up the band and going back into radio where he had been a very big success as a soloist. But John Hammond asked him to keep the band together and said that he would help him. He landed Benny and his band a job at NBC, broadcasting coast-to-coast. Benny was able to get Gene Krupa, who was receiving a lot of publicity at that time. Not long after Benny got the job, Hammond suggested using Teddy Wilson and Lionel Hampton. Hammond gave Benny the idea of wiring headlines all over the country that read in large letters, "Benny Goodman Hires Two Black Musicians." The publicity he received from that made him world-renowned.

Of course, Benny would have made it anyway because he was a super player and had a good band, but he made it playing all the old Fletcher Henderson arrangements. The charts were brown with age. It was incredible that we were playing all the same note-for-note arrangements that Fletcher had played all those years before that. It was primarily on the strength of Henderson's charts that Benny got the title "King of Swing." That was ridiculous. If anyone deserved the title it was Henderson.

Benny was not the most beloved bandleader. Indeed, he did not seem to know that anybody else existed. Yank Lawson told me about a time the band was at the Chicago Theater, which had a stage that rose out of a pit, higher than the average stage. After each show the guys would run to the closest bar and by the last show they'd be smashed. Hank D'Amico, a fine alto player and clarinetist, came back drunk one night. When the stage came down after the last show, the lights went off. It was difficult to see in that dark, even if one was sober. Hank slipped and fell, hitting his head on the side of the stage, and his clarinet went sliding along it. As he lay there in a state of semiconsciousness, Benny leaped over his fallen body, picked up the clarinet, played a few scales on it, and said, "The clarinet's okay, fellas! The clarinet's okay!"

When we were kids Benny was a wonderful guy, but he was a genius, and no genius can really handle a band and remain a good guy. Benny was not cruel, he just lived in a kind of egomaniacal shell. Working for Benny was the most miserable experience of my life. I was tired of big band factory work, tired of Benny, tired of playing "One O'Clock Jump" at 9 A.M. with a hangover. I wanted to play the music I loved, and as much of it as I wanted. After spending a year with Benny I went on a three-day drunk. When I came back the manager said, "I'm sorry to tell you that Benny wants you to take your notice." I said, "Well, I don't want to stay for the notice." I got them a tenor man, Jerry Jerome, and left in a few days. That was in 1938. I vowed I would never again work for someone else.

Bud Freeman (right) and Floyd O'Brien at White City Amusement Park in 1926.

In Dowagiac, Michigan, 1930. Left to right (standing): Vic Abbs, Jess Stacy, Bud Freeman, Dick McPartland; (seated): unidentified man, "Sleepy" Kaplan.

The Tommy Dorsey Clambake Seven at the St. Regis Hotel, 1938. Left to right: Tommy Dorsey, Bud Freeman, Yank Lawson, Carmen Mastren, Dave Tough, Artie Shapiro. Pianist Howard Smith is not shown. *Frank Driggs Collection. Used by permission.*

The Benny Goodman Band in Dayton, Ohio, 1938. Left to right: Bud Freeman, Noni Bernardi, Dave Matthews, Art Rollini, Martha Tilton (vocalist), Benny Goodman. Ben Heller and several other members of the band are not shown. *Frank Driggs Collection. Used by permission.*

From a 1938 Commodore album: Jess Stacy (piano), Jack Teagarden (trombone), Bobby Hackett (trumpet), Bud Freeman (tenor sax), Pee Wee Russell (clarinet), Eddie Condon (guitar), Artie Shapiro (bass), George Wettling (drums), (?) Bridges (recording engineer). *Composite by George A. Douglas. Used by permission of Milt Gabler of Commodore Record Co., Inc.*

Members of the Austin High Gang receive their varsity "A" at a reunion in 1942. Left to right: Jim Lannigan, Dick McPartland, Bud Freeman, and Mr. Summers, the principal of Austin High School. *Photo by Rube Lewis. Used by permission of* Down Beat *magazine.*

Bud and Estilita Freeman at the Onyx Club, 1943. *Used by permission of* Down Beat *magazine.*

Jimmy and Dick McPartland, late 1950s. *Used by permission of* Down Beat *magazine.*

Bud Freeman at an RCA recording session, 1957. *Used by permission of* Down Beat *magazine.*

Yank Lawson, Bob Haggart, and Bud Freeman at a JAM session in Indianapolis, 1986.

Johnny Mince, Bud Freeman, and Eddie Miller at an Allegheny Jazz Society festival in Lake Conneaut, Pennsylvania, 1986.

CHAPTER | F I V E

"Beat to the Socks"

During the end of my tenure with the Goodman band we were playing at the Waldorf-Astoria. I did an occasional record for Commodore, and, in fact, shortly before leaving Goodman I was recording a parody of Noel Coward's *Private Lives* which Commodore was producing. The parody was written by Johnny DeVries (Peter DeVries's brother) and was called *Private Jives*. Minerva Pious, the commedienne who played Mrs. Nusbaum on the "Fred Allen Show," was reading the female lead opposite me. We were playing two jaded sophisticates. She asks me, "How are you feeling?" I say, "Distended, my dearest. I do feel rather like a small paper bag filled with an unpleasant subway breathe. What hour is it?" "Tenish." "Oh gad, I thought it was fivish." Later on we talk about a character named Cockeye. "How is Cockeye?" she asks. "Cockeye says your lips are like two thin strips of wet liver." Minerva's character is supposed to be playing cornet, but we had Joe Bushkin dub it for her. I say, "Gad, how you do carry on," and she says, "I must practice, I have five shows tomorrow." We had a gas with that record, which I heard became something of a collector's item. John Huston, Noel Coward, and the Duke of Windsor all had copies.

We used to rehearse the play at Minerva's, and to get to her reading room where we rehearsed we had to pass through her bedroom. One early evening I saw this well-dressed, dapper-looking fellow lying on her bed with a bowler over his face and a cane alongside him. He said his name was Ernie Anderson. He was very friendly, but we didn't say very much then; I did learn, however, that even though he did not speak

French he had just come back from Paris where he had been working for an American magazine.

Ernie was staying up late every night, hanging out in the Village at Nick's Sizzling Steaks, listening to jazz. He was a graduate of MIT but was not the scientific type; he wanted to do something in the arts. During the day he was a copywriter for an advertising agency, Young and Rubicam, and he hated it. The head of the agency loved Ernie, and I remember going over there one day to see him and there was a message from his boss that said, "Ernie, don't you like it here anymore?" We went into his boss's office and Ernie said, "I've been thinking of leaving," and he quit right then and there. He had a beautiful apartment on Park Avenue and lived a luxurious life but gave it all up to become an impressario.

He began by handling Eddie Condon. He couldn't have picked a worse guy because Eddie was drunk all the time. Even so he made Eddie famous, though he never got anything out of it himself. Ernie got Eddie numerous Town Hall concerts and had all the top journalists from the leading New York papers doing pieces on Eddie. He even got Virgil Thompson to write one for the *New York Times*. Ernie couldn't do anything for himself, but he could do a lot for an artist if he liked him. He didn't make any money until years later, when he started handling John Huston.

I introduced Ernie to Eddie. By an odd coincidence Eddie's wife, Phyllis, was also a copywriter for Young and Rubicam. I had met her through her brother, Paul Smith, an artist whom I had met in New York City in 1933 when I was playing with Ray Noble. When Paul went away for the summer I took his apartment for three months. Phyllis came to New York and Paul got her a job with Young and Rubicam. I introduced Phyllis to Eddie and they eventually married and had two daughters. Even though Ernie got Eddie a tremendous amount of publicity in those days, Phyllis supported Eddie throughout the late thirties and early forties, until he opened his club in 1946.

When he first went to work for Eddie, Ernie began getting a lot of publicity for me. I was rehearsing an eighteen-piece big band and he had us in national magazines. I was in *Esquire, Fortune,* and *Vanity Fair.* In fact, I did a modeling job for *Vanity Fair.* I had a big head of hair then and was well dressed and looked like a well-to-do guy, or at least like a clothes model. Underneath my photo it said, "What does this man do? He's a jazz musician."

In the meantime I was getting fed up with my band. We did a two-week tour of fifteen New England cities and I knew I wasn't cut out to be a bandleader. A successful bandleader doesn't give a damn about his musicians—he can't afford to; he's got to be tough as nails, but I couldn't manage that. Besides, the big-band era was about over and work was getting scarce. I told Ernie how I felt and he said, "Look, you've had a tremendous amount of publicity, would you want to front Eddie's band?"

Condon's band was at Nick's Sizzling Steaks, an expensive restaurant in the Village that catered to wealthy college kids and celebrities— writers, painters, composers, and conductors. They all loved the band. Nick was a kind of a ragtime piano player, but he liked jazz music and somebody had talked him into taking in Condon's group—Pee Wee Russell, Max Kaminsky, Brad Gowans, and all of them. They were doing very well; they were causing a big stir and had been since the days I was with Dorsey. Whenever I had been in town with the Dorsey band I would go down and sit in with them. I told Ernie, "Yes, I'd like to front the band, but I don't want to have any headaches other than to play." I signed a contract to that effect and they put me in front of the band, which Phyllis called Bud Freeman and the Summa Cum Laude. Our opening night at Nick's was sold out. A lot of the big recording people came down, including some from RCA who liked us and eventually signed us for quite a few recording dates.

We were at Nick's for about six or seven months when we got an offer to do a Broadway show called "Swingin' the Dream." The show was produced by Eric Charell, who had had tremendous success in Europe with a show called "White Horse Inn." He came to America with enormous financial backing to create a revue mixing *Midsummer Night's Dream* with black vaudeville. He had just about the finest talent you could get. Just about everyone in the show became world-renowned. He had Louis Armstrong, Nicodemus, Troy Brown, Oscar Polk, Butterfly McQueen, Bill Bailey, Dorothy Maguire, and Maxine Sullivan. If Charell had known the greatness of the black people he could have had a revue that would still be running.

There was some excellent music in the show. Jimmy Van Heusen wrote a number of pieces for it, and one of them, "Darn That Dream," has become a classic. The show also had two excellent bands, ours and Benny Goodman's. Benny's sextet, with Fletcher Henderson on piano and Charlie Christian on guitar, was in a loge on the left side of the theater and ours was in a loge on the right. The two bands played for fifteen minutes before the curtain went up.

Despite this talent the show was headed for disaster, but we were oblivious to it. The manager, who was a friendly guy, made us an offer. He said, "Bud, what are you doing in this show? This is going to fold." He offered us money if we wanted to get out, but Ernie said, "No, let's turn it down." He thought it could be a great hit. As it turned out we never got paid for any of it. That show ran about eleven days and we found ourselves out of work.

The next job we took was in a real rough dive, sort of an under-world rendezvous on Forty-seventh Street, between Sixth and Seventh avenues. The boss was a jailbird and limped as though he had been carrying a ball and chain on his right leg all his life. But he was a nice guy, and somebody sold him on the idea of taking us in. We had a following of rich people, show people, and journalists, and when he saw them he partitioned the front of the place, which was the rendezvous for the underworld characters, and let the others into the back room to hear the jazz. We were working for about thirty-seven dollars a week, anything to keep the band together.

All the people who worked for this underworld character had been in jail, including the doorman, who had just been released. He was a pick-pocket. On opening night I heard the boss say, "Now, Jimmy, be careful, I don't want you picking anybody's pockets. These are elegant people and I don't want any trouble." Jimmy said, "Gee, boss, I won't have no fun."

John O'Hara, who had written *Appointment in Samara* and *Butterfield 8*, was a regular at this place. He was one of those awful drunks who goes completely out of his mind when he's on a binge; John was a true roughhouse Irishman who liked to fight. But he was a jazz fan, and he had written a book of short stories called *Hat on the Bed* that included "The Flatted Saxophone," about a society party the protagonist goes to in Philadelphia. The host asks him to come in and hear the music. It's that sobbing, melodic, sentimental, tenor saxophone lead, and the pro-tagonist says, "If I want to hear a good saxophone, I'll find out where Bud Freeman's playing," which was a tremendous plug!

Anyway, wherever we played John would come around and start a fight. I was always able to handle him because, as drunk as he'd be, he always seemed to know me and I could get him out of the place. John came in terribly drunk one night to this underworld rendezvous, and got into an argument with one of the hoodlums. I was watching all of this from the bandstand. I ran over with my saxophone, so that the hoodlum would know I was a musician. I yelled, "Stop! Don't hurt this man! This is John O'Hara, the great novelist." The hoodlum turned to me and paused, just before the boss came running over, yelling, "Don't touch that man! He's different from us!"

We had played there a few months when Willard Alexander booked us into the Panther Room at the Sherman Hotel in Chicago to play a show with Lee Wiley, the singer, and Stuff Smith, the jazz violinist. Squirrel Ashcraft, a jazz aficionado who had helped Benny Goodman in Chicago, got us the job. We had a ball out there for about a month, alternating with Stuff Smith's band. Every night I would do a number in front of his band and he would do one in front of mine. After that Bud Freeman and the Summa Cum Laude went back to New York, where we broke up. Jazz music is the only kind of music that can take its players from rags to riches to rags in one month.

Ernie and I then shared a room at the Forest Hotel, a theatrical fleabag on Forty-ninth Street between Broadway and Eighth Avenue. Times were hard. I wasn't doing anything and neither was Ernie. We were there about a month and broke almost all the time. Curiously, I was not worried about money. I never have been, until I've had some. Across the street from the hotel was a funny little Greek restaurant where we used to eat roast pork with apple sauce. It was a hangout for show people. It was clean but kind of down at the heels, one of those places where the waiters yell back to the chef. The first time I ordered the roast pork the waiter hollered, "Hey, chef! I wanna roast pork or apple sauce!" As soon as we got hold of any money we went to a good place.

How we managed to survive eating all that horrible food, I don't know. Someone told us it was better to eat some food, no matter how bad it tasted, than nothing. But since we were dead broke most of our stay there, we went days at a time without eating. When I got a royalty check from ASCAP for twenty-five dollars I said to Ernie, "What's the best restaurant in town?" He said, "The Brussels." We went there. For twenty-five dollars we bought a great meal for both of us and the next day we didn't have enough money to walk outside.

Our stay at the Forest Hotel soon came to an end. Ernie took a job with another ad agency and I put together a sextet with Max Kaminsky on trumpet, Dave Bowman on piano, Brad Gowans on trombone, Al Druten on alto and clarinet, and Jim Donahue on drums. Donahue replaced Dave Tough, who had played with us for about a week and then stopped showing up. Dave was drinking heavily. We went on the road and did about twenty-one one-nighters. We weren't making any money, just struggling to hold on.

We soon broke up and in 1940 I got an offer to go to Florida into a Miami club run by the Jewish mob. I took piano player Bill Clifton and drummer Al Sidell with me. After about two weeks I came down with a horrible flu that knocked me out for another two weeks. The mob, believe it or not, paid me for the two weeks I didn't work.

Arny sent for me then, and while I was staying with him in Chicago, Wingy Manone, who was playing at the Brass Rail, was let go and the owners asked me if I would like to put a group in. I had met Wingy back in the twenties when I had worked for him at the Merry Gardens in Chicago. I was playing the C-melody then and I had gotten the job along with Tesch. Wingy and I got along very well. He was a one-armed cornet player who had spent a lot of time in the twenties hanging out with Louis Armstrong on the South Side and he played with Louis's beat.

Wingy had lost his arm in New Orleans; I heard that he had fallen under a streetcar as a young boy. At any rate, "Wingy" was the nickname for one-armed guys in New Orleans and Manone got stuck with the moniker. He knew the hard side of life; no one was going to put one over on him. There's a rouse that pimps and whores play in hotels. I believe it's called the Badger Game. The whore picks up a guy in a hotel lobby and her accomplice follows them upstairs and waits until the guy is undressed, then bursts into the room and they rob him. When a whore and her pimp tried pulling this on Wingy he ended up robbing them. There were not many underhanded things that Wingy didn't know about.

Yank Lawson told me that back in the twenties Wingy was playing in a restaurant in Louisville, Kentucky; the owner was an old southern colonel. Wingy was playing loudly, and one night the owner said, "Mr. Manone, I'd appreciate it if you would put in the mute during dinner so the people can converse." Wingy refused to comply, so the colonel came back and said, "I am sorry, Mr. Manone, but I have no choice but to fire you." Ordinarily Wingy would have killed someone for saying such a thing to him, but in this case he simply said, "Colonel, suh, I'll be a muthafuckah. This is *indeed* a surprise."

Once again my tenure as a bandleader did not last very long. We had a good outfit at the Brass Rail and we had a following among Gold Coast jazz fans. All the famous bandleaders would come in when they were in town. Still, the guys would show up late because I was a friend, not a leader; I wasn't the kind of guy who could fire them. The owners were continually complaining to me about tardiness. Of course, they held me responsible for the fact that these guys were straggling in a half hour or even an hour after the first set started. I didn't want the responsibility, so I went to the guys and said, "Do you want to quit?" and they said, "No." They shaped up for a month but then went back to their old habits. Finally, after four months I told the owners that was it and when the band came in that night I said, "Boys, we've just given notice." They hit the ceiling, but I didn't care. I was fed up. They had no idea they'd all lose their jobs; they must have figured that at worst I would fire a few of them and hire replacements.

I had a guy by the name of Bill Dohler in the band, a very fine, elegant alto player who still lives in Chicago. In fact, he lived a block away from me when we were kids, but I never knew him until I was eighteen. I met him when we played together at a fraternity dance in Chicago. We became good friends, but I never knew how wild he was until we played the Brass Rail together.

Each night after we finished our last set there, Bill and I would go over to the Ohio Inn, which was open twenty-four hours a day, for some drinks and late food. One night Bill said, "Look, let's take some popcorn and feed the animals at the zoo. They come out about 7:30 in the morning." So we walked all the way up to Lincoln Park Zoo. Bill jumped over a rail and began feeding the polar bear. Now, incredibly enough, the polar bear ate the food off Bill's hand without scratching a finger. Elated with his success, Bill moved to the the next cage, which held a big female grizzly. He dug his hand into his bag of popcorn, came up with a fistful, and thrust it between the bars. The grizzly lumbered up and took a big bite but got hold of more than popcorn. She dug her teeth into three of Bill's fingers and he damn near lost them. It took about six weeks for them to heal. He brooded about this incident for months, and early one morning, as he sat nursing his grudge with a fifth of bourbon, he got an inspiration for revenge. He took one of this golf clubs and went looking for the grizzly. He managed to entice her over to the bars, then whacked her over the head with the club. Bill said that as she was going down she had a guilty look on her face.

Right after I broke up the band at the Brass Rail, Bill took me to see Ray O'Hara, who booked the North Shore society dates. The idea, which O'Hara bought, was that I would put together a big band for these jobs. Even though they were society dates we never played society music; we always played what we liked and the people loved it. Ours was sort of a rehearsal band. We had different arrangers and a lot of times we would get a date for just six musicians. In those days we had to play popular tunes, but we didn't play them the way a society band would. We were playing for ourselves; fortunately, it was a very lucrative field. After two years of that I moved the band into the Panther Room at the Sherman Hotel.

By 1942 guys were being inducted into the service left and right. Bill was not enthusiastic about the prospect of going in, and he thought I ought to stay out too. He kept telling me, "Bud, you'd better do something about staying out of the army. You'll never be able to take it." Bill had his own idea of how he'd keep out. When he was about ten years old he had been run over by a car while riding his bicycle. That had left a very big dent in his leg. Now when he got his notice to report to his draft board he got very drunk one night and took a golf club and banged the dent. The leg swelled up and he bought some crutches and went down to the draft board. Believe it or not they took him in. As it was, I ended up a model soldier in the Aleutian Islands and he ended up in Florida playing golf for four years.

For as long as he was in the army Bill refused to salute any officer or to say, "Yes, sir," so they always had him on reprimand. One day a general came in and really laced him down. He said, "Stand at attention. Isn't there something you're supposed to say to an officer?" Bill didn't say a word, so the general roared, "What's your name?" Now for some inexplicable reason Bill has always used two names. The government knows him as William Hildebrand, but in music he's known as Bill Dohler. So when the general yelled, "What's your name?" Bill gave him a very smart salute and said, "Sir William Hildebrand."

Bill is still active in music. He's the big thing for Chinese funerals in Chicago now. He's got a big band, and the Chinese love big American dance bands at their funerals.

"The Atomic Era"

I stayed out of the war until 1943. Everybody was in uniform and I felt embarrassed being in civilian clothes. I was thirty-six, playing in the Panther Room, when I was finally drafted.

Just before I got my notice I met my first wife, Estilita. I was sitting in a bar one night and she came in with her date, some rich Chicago Gold Coast guy, and she left him to come over to say hello to me. She had very dark hair, beautiful blue eyes, a very light complexion, and a lovely figure. She said, "You may not remember me, but I met you with my ex-husband, who's a fan of yours." I said, "Oh, yes, I remember you very well." We got to talking and she went back to her date and suddenly I saw him leave. She came back and said, "I've just sent my date away." We spent the rest of the evening together.

She was a knockout, a real Italian beauty. That's what attracted me to her, not the fact that she was kind and loyal, which I didn't find out until later. All I saw in her then was her figure, her elegant clothes, and her joie de vivre. She must have seen something in me because within two weeks we were engaged.

Shortly thereafter I was sent to Camp Grant, in Rockford, Illinois, and everybody seemed to know me because of the band at the Sherman Hotel. So instead of putting me on all the hard details like shoveling coal and garbage they made me the leader of a post band. Different famous acts would come in and we'd play their music. They kept me there for a month and then sent me to Fort Meade, where I began five months of combat basic training.

It was the real thing, gas masks and all that, including infiltration exercises, where we crawled under live bullets and over mines. The mines weren't all that strong, but some did explode and they could shock you. I must say, though, that I came to love basic training. I'd never felt so healthy in my life. For one thing I stopped drinking. The food wasn't that good, of course, so I didn't eat very much and became pretty hard.

I was in the 38th Special Service Company. A special service company was a small company (we had 118 men) and its job was to go into the war areas and entertain the soldiers or bring things to them. I had a friend in Washington, a major or colonel, and he requisitioned a lot of guys from big bands as they came into the service and sent them to me. This band had twenty excellent musicians and some brilliant arrangements. I fronted it only because I was the name. The musicians were all terribly unhappy when they found out we were going to the Aleutian Islands because they all had hoped to end up in Europe. I had wanted to be sent there too. Just before they sent us to Alaska, they gave me a week's furlough so I could get married.

I was made a T-4, which was equivalent to a buck sergeant. Being a bandleader I had the same privileges as a warrant officer. I had entrée to all the officers clubs. When we were in the Aleutian Islands they didn't really have anything for us to do, so we made a show called "Take a Break" and toured the Aleutian chain and then went to the Alaskan mainland for about a month. It was a very good show. It was very clever. Incidentally, we were based on Adak in the Aleutians.

The famous detective story writer Dashiell Hammett had a newspaper called the *Adakian*. He was a very brilliant man, and he was allowed to write pretty much what he liked in his editorials. He rarely wrote anything about our own troops but he did write a lot about the Russians. The head of the Alaskan command came down to see Hammett about this. Now Hammett was a buck sergeant. He refused to be anything more because he didn't have to be in the Army. He had had tuberculosis, which he cured himself, but he wanted to help in some way so there he was in the Aleutian Islands. The general came, not to reprimand him, but to ask him why he wrote these articles. He said, "Sergeant Hammett, why do we not have any word about the progress of the American forces? All you write about is the Russians."

Now at that particular time some officers, including generals, colonels, and majors, had raided three or four boxcars in Germany that were filled with cigarettes. They stole these cigarettes and were selling them to the Russian soldiers for about fifty dollars a carton. It was an incredible scandal, and Hammett had published a piece on it. So he said to the general, "General, our newspaper, the *Adakian,* has a policy not to publish any advertising." The general threw up his hands and left. They had tremendous respect for Hammett. I think he was making at least a hundred thousand dollars a year from his films and books, and if there is anything a general admires it's the ability to make money. They don't make very much of it, or they didn't, I'm sure, during the war — outside of that scandal we heard about.

Our troops were running plenty of other scams. They were selling Mickey Mouse watches to the Russian soldiers for a tremendous amount of money. Then there was a naval base on Adak where a lot of merchant marines were bringing in booze. The MP's would give them so much a case for the booze and then resell it. We had a lot of civilians working there. The MP's were selling bottles of Old Grandad to them and to the soldiers for as high as $100 or $150 a bottle. There was an awful lot of rum running going on. People were making a lot of money from that. In fact, there was one guy who sent home enough money to open up a night-club in a little town in the United States. And then you had a lot of card sharks up there running poker games. It was incredible.

Oh, they were cleaning up. They had ways of sending money home. There were a lot of rackets going on, but I stayed out of all of that. I was very thankful to have the band and not have anybody shooting at me. With all the basic training I had I saw no action at all. We didn't get there until 1943, and the Japanese had been out of there, it seems to me, since the end of 1941.

There's an interesting thing about music in the war. We had some brilliant arrangers and some of us had played a lot of jazz in the big bands. The army used our band to play host theaters on the mainland and the islands and whenever something was going wrong with the company. If some top brass was a little upset with our C.O., our C.O. would say, "Get the band out." About six officers would come over and we'd charm them with the band. We'd pretend we were having a rehearsal. It always worked. The music always saved things for us. A most incredible thing, the power of American dance music. There were radar men who had been stuck in the Aleutian Islands for some four years, since the inception of the Japanese trouble, and they would break down and cry when they heard the band, they loved it so much.

It was in Alaska that I found out an interesting thing about being commercial. I discovered that people don't listen as much as they look. We were doing a show on one of the little islands on the chain. We were playing in the mess hall, and we were doing our best playing but it didn't seem to be going over so well. These were a lot of bitter men who had been stuck up there a long time and they just defied us to entertain them. Now we were dressed in heavy Arctic equipment and looked like a bunch of Eskimos. It wasn't that it was so terribly cold there, but this was our way of dressing. You could fall down and not get hurt because the clothing was so thickly padded.

I used to play a solo, about ten improvised choruses, on "I Got Rhythm," and suddenly during my solo the idea came to me just to fall back and not break the motion of the play, just to fall back. So I fell on my back with my feet up in the air and some of the men jumped up. They were completely out of their minds. "This is the greatest fuckin' saxophone player in the world," they were screaming. If I had wanted to become a clown I could have made a million dollars. I never used gimmicks, though. I've always taken my music quite seriously. I like to have humor in what I do, but there was an example of what your real audience likes. The guys said, "How in the hell can a guy play a saxophone on his back?" They didn't know that I was clowning. They thought I was being serious about it. Somehow or other this showmanship reaches the people. It'll always be that way, let's face it. That was the first and last time I ever used a stunt like that. I was just trying to find out something.

That brings to mind a marvelous story about a gay major in the 11th Air Command on Adak, a very effeminate little man. I don't know that he got into any trouble. He was, I suppose, pretty careful. Now we used to break up the big band into little bands and go around and play at officers clubs, which we were paid to do. One night this major called me and said, "Sergeant Freeman, would you want to bring a little group over to play for my company?" I said, "Yes, I'd be delighted," and he said, "We'll pay you well for it." So I brought over a six-piece band. He had a little nightclub with a dance floor set up in this mess hall. It was candlelit and set up for couples. There were no women there. The nurses, who were not the most attractive people, didn't come to the thing. Now everybody got sort of drunk and the officers got up and danced with one another. They weren't gay, there just weren't any women there to dance with. The piano player in my group, who was not gay but very drunk, got up and danced with the major.

The general, or some very important officer, heard about it the next day and came over and reprimanded the little gay major because he had heard about the officers dancing with one another. So they put up a sign that read, "In Future, Enlisted Men Will Not Dance With Officers At Any Of The Dances Or Parties." A few months later the little major called me up and said, "Freeman, I'd like to hire your group to play for another party." So the band went over and just before we began to play the major put a note in my hand that read, "Freeman, will you make sure that the men in the group do not get drunk this time because we have an order that the enlisted men are not to dance with officers." At the bottom he had written, "You know, Freeman, I don't mind, but the General just doesn't understand." The guy thought I was gay.

There was an interesting thing about the blacks and the whites on the island. There was a black cannon company, probably one of the best in the service. There were also a lot of very prejudiced white people on the islands, and occasionally there were small outbreaks of trouble. Finally the band got together and said, "Why don't we go and play for these black troops?" We had a couple of very prejudiced sergeants in our company, very ignorant men, and they resented the idea. But we took our show over anyway and played for this cannon company and they really loved it. They said it was a good band and had a lot of beautiful arrangements, and we made a lot of friends. Several times when I was walking along the road they saw me and picked me up and took me over to their mess hall for dinner. It was a great feeling to make friends with them.

The prejudice that existed in the service was tremendous because we had a lot of southern soldiers who were poorly educated and had been taught that the black man was some creature that didn't belong with the rest of us. It was a terrible thing. I felt sorry for the black people who had to serve in the South. It must have been awful. I don't know how things were in Europe, but I understand that there could have been some difficulty for black soldiers. I wasn't there, so I don't know. But there could have been a lot of trouble in the islands if we hadn't gotten together and had the jam sessions and the shows. I was very lucky that I was in a very intelligent company.

Jazz music has done so much to bring people together. I saw it there in the islands. I mean I could walk into any black mess hall and get a meal. They were marvelous to us because they realized we cared. I don't mean to say that we were doing anything great, we were just doing something human. And do you know that I ran into many of those black soldiers after the war in different towns during tours and they would come backstage to see me. I've never forgotten that.

"Jack Hits the Road"

I was thirty-nine in 1945 when the army sent me back to the States on furlough and for a change of station. We flew from Anchorage to Minneapolis, and on the plane was a heavily bemedaled war hero. We got to talking, and suddenly we hit some bad air pockets and the plane dropped a thousand feet. I wasn't frightened because I had done so much flying in the Aleutians, where I would be up two or three days a week in a heavy wind flying almost upside down. But this hero was down on his knees, quivering and praying. I put my arm around him and said, "Come on, this is nothing. We're going to make it. Come on, get up. After what you've been through, why should you be frightened of this?"

He lived in the Deep South somewhere and they wanted to fly him from Minneapolis to his home, but he refused to get on the plane. They said, "Well, it'll take you a helluva long time to get home on the trains." The trains were jammed with guys moving around after coming back from the war. They said it might take him three or four days to get home. He said, "I don't give a damn. I'm not going to get on a plane again."

I took a train from Minneapolis to New York because Estilita was living there. I stayed about a week in New York, and while I was there I learned that we had dropped the atomic bombs on Japan and lowered the service age to thirty-eight. I received orders to go to Fort Dix, where I was mustered out in three days. Those were the longest three days I ever spent in the service. I was in with a bunch of paratroopers who should have been sent through hospitals. Half of them were crazy. They burned down one of the barracks, knocked down the fences, went into town and went completely out of their minds. This went on for three days. I hid.

I'll never forget the day I got out. There was a little colonel handing us our diplomas, as we called them, our honorary discharges. This little colonel was saluting everybody. He might have saluted a thousand guys in one day, and it was very hot. It was in August. I said to him, "Colonel, you don't have to salute me." That broke him up. He was a little bit of a man and we were having a rough time in that heat. I'll never forget what a thrill it was getting out. I was in O.D.'s, the winter outfit, and they gave me these suntans, which gave me a lift.

Something strange had happened to me while I was in the army. Over the course of the three years I was in I had lost confidence in my playing. After being discharged I went to all kinds of teachers but each of them was trying to sell himself and I was becoming confused. Then I heard about a blind pianist named Lennie Tristano and I said, "He'll know what my problem is." I thought that a brilliant musician who was blind would certainly hear what was wrong, and he did. He listened to me play and he said, "Man, you're tight as a drum."

Some critics have said that Lennie was teaching me the elements of his own style, but he wasn't. He didn't want to change my style; he seemed to like it. We just played together. In one month he had my confidence back, and one day when I started to get this big sound he said, "That's great!" This was years before he made a name for himself, when he was just making his living teaching. My problem, by the way, was not unique. Lots of musicians have been plagued with it, including a famous trumpet player with the New York Philharmonic. It even happened to Benny Goodman for a couple of months.

During my stint in the service I didn't see Estilita for twenty-eight months, and when I came back we didn't know each other. In fact, we had hardly known each other before the war. Now I found out that I wasn't in love with her. Lots of others were taken by her, though, especially men. As I said, she was quite gorgeous and always beautifully dressed because her sister was a professional clothing designer. Men chased her all the time and she'd become furious with me because I didn't care. "You bastard," she'd yell, "you don't give a damn who flirts with me!" She had a real Italian temperament. Wherever we went, especially Italian restaurants, people knew her and we'd end up at their tables. We often went to the Grotto Azura, which was a hangout for a lot of opera singers, including Lawrence Tibbett. Estilita knew all of them.

The first job I had after the war was as the house bandleader for Majestic Records. Ernie Anderson called me about the job. The ex-mayor of New York, Jimmy Walker, was vice president of the company. During my time at Majestic I recorded what may have been the first free jazz improvisation. I made it with drummer Ray McKinley and called it "The Atomic Era." I was free-lancing around New York then, recording and playing jazz parties at Ivy League schools. When Bing Crosby came to town that year for a recording date he asked for me. Billy Butterfield and Joe Bushkin were also on the session, and I remember that Bing loved it. Jobs were not that frequent, though, and when Majestic Records closed, Estilita and I had no money.

At that time there were about twelve jazz clubs between Fifth and Sixth avenues on Fifty-second Street in New York. It was an exciting block; I've never seen anything else like it, not even in Chicago in the twenties. People would go from one club to another and listen to jazz for maybe five or six hours. It was a way of life.

When the jazz clubs first started popping up on Fifty-second Street they were surrounded by a lot of strip joints. The owners of the strip joints were rightly worried that the jazz clubs were going to take away their business. Indeed, more jazz clubs kept opening, and there was a real carnival atmosphere there. People would go from one club to another to hear it all. There was money around in those days.

In 1946 I got a call from the man who ran Jimmy Ryan's on Fifty-second Street. He said, "What do you play? Do you play Chicago? Do you play bebop? Do you play New Orleans? What?" And I said, "I play beautifully." He broke up laughing and I went in. I organized a trio that included Denzil Best, a fine bebop drummer who admired Dave Tough. It wasn't all that odd for me to be playing with a bebop rhythm section. Lester Young didn't play Charlie Parker's and Dizzy Gillespie's style but he used to play with a bebop rhythm section. Coleman Hawkins played with those same rhythm sections too. So did Ben Webster. If you had a name, you worked, and so I worked all through the bebop era. I was in the jazz field as a soloist.

A lot of great talent was working on Fifty-second Street then. Jack Teagarden had a band at a club across the street from Jimmy Ryan's. He didn't like his bosses, and one hot summer night he came out of his club, perspiring and carrying his trombone, and walked over to my club and played a whole set with me. Red Allen and J. C. Higginbotham were also playing on the other side of the street, and they once walked out of their club and came over and played a whole set with me. James Moody, Dizzy Gillespie's sax player, would come over and sit in. Oh, it was fantastic in those days.

Part of the fun was that musicians had no regard for categories, and players with different styles would work together. Bebop musicians didn't call themselves bebop musicians. Dizzy Gillespie told me, "We didn't call it that. Some critic must have given it the name." "Bebop" was a word Louis Armstrong sang in the middle of a chorus on a record date. He was holding up the music to read the lyric and dropped the sheet. Rather than spoil the take he began scat singing. Scat singing has no words, just sounds, and "bebop" was one of the sounds Louis sang.

There were a lot of very talented people who came along in that era who were categorized as old-fashioned if they did not play the new music and could not get work if they didn't. It never affected me because I was well known and could always work, but it did hurt a lot of musicians. I think that "Hot Lips" Page, one of the great gut-bucket trumpet players of our time, died broken-hearted. He just couldn't cope with it.

Long before the bebop era Biederbecke had been listening to Stravinsky, Ravel, Ebert, Scriabin, and others. The beboppers drew their chords from these composers, but no jazz musician before Biederbecke had an understanding of so-called modern harmony. When this bebop era came along the music was already old to the people who knew Bix and those composers. I don't mean to put down the creators of that style. Charlie Parker was a true genius and Dizzy Gillespie was some sort of genius. I just resented all their imitators because they weren't good enough musicians to play what they were trying to play, which was what Dizzy and Charlie played. When I first heard Bud Powell play I said, "This is what these guys are trying to play." The people who played it best were those who were already recognized, who had come out of the big band era, like Dizzy and Charlie and Clark Terry and Sonny Stitt. I think the best player in that style was Stan Getz because he always had an understanding of melodic line, whereas a lot of these players never knew where the melody was.

There were a thousand untalented musicians trying to play it. Most not only didn't have a sense of melodic line, most hadn't any beat in their bodies. They completely skipped the wonderful music of King Oliver and Louis. They didn't know it because if they had, and had the feeling for the wonderful beat that King Oliver, Louis, and the early black church singers had, some of that would have rubbed off on them. They might argue that they had no regard for the beat, but that couldn't be possible because once you feel this beat you can never get away from it. You wouldn't want to, it's such a marvelous way to play. Dizzy and Charlie knew where the beat was because they'd played in some bands that swung, but their imitators hadn't. I doubt very much if most of them felt anything. They used to stand with their feet together when they played. I didn't find this music very deep at all. When people asked me what I thought of it I always used to say, "I prefer Ravel and Debussy." I found them much deeper.

In February 1946 Eddie Condon opened a club down in the Village. It was called Eddie Condon's but he was fronting it for someone else. Eddie was going to close on Mondays, but Ernie Anderson told him that with all the publicity I had they should put me in with an all-star band. He did and I went in with tenor, clarinet, trumpet, drums, guitar, and piano. The personnel kept changing; I used whoever was available. Sometimes we had Joe Bushkin on piano, Bob Haggart on bass, Dave Tough on drums, "Hot Lips" Page or Billy Butterfield or Buck Clayton on trumpet. Tommy and Jimmy Dorsey used to come down and sit in. So did Jack Teagarden. All of the famous bandleaders, theater people, and artists came. John Steinbeck and Spencer Tracy, who were good friends, used to come; so did Jacob Epstein, the sculptor, Alexander King, an editor at *Life* magazine, and Joe DiMaggio, the great Yankee hitter. Famous writers on the *New Yorker* staff, including John O'Hara, used to frequent the place. It was always a sellout, but after a couple of months Eddie closed on Sundays and Mondays because union law said he could only have a five-day week.

Even after I left Eddie's times were very lucrative. Still, I left New York in 1947 to go to Brazil. One of the richest men in the world, Jorge Guinle, loved jazz and owned a place in Rio called the Midnight Room. He asked me if I would like to play it and I jumped at the chance. When he asked me what hours I wanted to play I said, "You called it the Midnight Room, so let's start at twelve." I took Joe Bushkin and a bass player named Herb Ward with me, and Guinle got a Portuguese drummer for us, a black guy named Bibi Miranda. He was a marvelous drummer. He had never worked with sticks, just with his fingers. Bibi used to say, "Hey, Buh Freeman, you no like white man. I feel so easy with you."

One time he invited Joe and me to his home. He'd never had any white people there. I told him I couldn't come that day and Joe just didn't show up. Bibi was so sensitive he thought it was because he was black. When I saw him next he pointed to his stomach and said, "I feel so bad, it make me feel that someone kick me here." Later I invited him to a very posh party for the richest people in Brazil and he said, "Oh, Buh Freeman, are you sure they won't talk to me?" I said, "They will, you're with me." When he saw them he said, "Look at all this rich people. They have everything, and they don't swing; we swing, we got shit."

We played for dancing at the Midnight Room and it was a tremendous success. The deposed king of Yugoslavia, an obese playboy named Carol, and Magda Lupescu, his mistress, had come to Brazil to live and they used to frequent the room. Guinle offered me a two-year contract to stay, but after four months there Estilita broke out with boils all over her body. She had contracted a local disease called *ouchichia* (or something like that) and we all came back.

Estilita and I moved into a hotel in New York City. I played occasionally at Condon's and eventually got an offer to go with the Condon all-star group to the Blue Note in Chicago. We had Peanuts Hucko on clarinet, me on tenor, Eddie on guitar, Zutty Singleton on drums, Pete Peterson on bass, and Bobby Hackett on trumpet. When the job ended they went back to New York, but Estilita and I stayed because we had found a nice apartment in Chicago. Dave Garroway was hiring talent for the Blue Note, and in 1948 he asked me if I would stay on in partnership with Jimmy and Marian McPartland.

Jimmy had met Marian in Europe during the war, when he had been a driver for an officer. The officer, who was a jazz fan, knew who Jimmy was and had requested him. Marian was playing piano for the U.S.O., and she talked Jimmy into joining it after his discharge. They got married in Europe but came here and Marian became an American citizen. Our date at the Blue Note—we had a seven-piece band—was supposed to be for a month, but they kept us for four. When that ended Jimmy and Marian went back East and I stayed around Chicago.

I was in Chicago when I heard that Dave Tough had been found dead on a street in Newark, New Jersey. He'd been living there with his black wife when he was robbed and killed. There were many stories about how he died; I don't know if any of them are true, but I did hear that his body lay in a morgue for three days before his wife identified it. I was saddened by his death but not shocked because it seemed that he'd been trying to kill himself for most of his life. He'd been drinking since he was fifteen and had simply burnt himself out. He did have periods of sobriety—at one time he didn't drink for three years—but then he'd get sick of it all and go on an endless drunk and wouldn't eat. He went through hell the last year of his life, and when I heard that he'd died I just thought, Well, he's over all his misery.

By the time Dave died my marriage had sort of petered out. Estilita and I were living at the Croydon Hotel when we separated in 1949. I wasn't working, though I could have; I just didn't like the jobs. We weren't happy. We'd always had a stormy marriage, though I never argued much. Estilita wanted me to have a band, but I didn't want that. I had this dream of becoming a soloist, which she couldn't understand. Still, she was really very good to me, kind and considerate; she was just upset with me because I didn't have any ambition. I was not a good husband, yet she actually cared about me. She'd get into great arguments about my playing, always defending me, always telling everybody what a gentleman I was. We did not separate in anger. She just went to live with her sister and I stayed on at the Croydon.

I wasn't making a living and didn't do anything for a hell of a long time until I met a woman named Margo. She owned eight restaurants in Chicago, all called Margo's. Her husband, who was supposed to be managing them, was an alcoholic, and since he didn't take care of them they started going downhill. By the time I met Margo she had only one left, in the skid row section of Madison Street. We fell in love and she said, "Look, you're not working, why don't you put a band in my dining room and we'll see if we can make a jazz club out of it?" We had a shot, we thought, because famous journalists used to come in there.

Soon after I moved a band in we got a notice saying our liquor license was about to be revoked. Spike Hennessey, my dear friend, was a jazz fan and politically well connected, so I called him up and he called the governor and got us a six-month stay on the license.

Since Margo was supporting me all this time I didn't take any pay from the band work, I just paid the men. We weren't doing very much business, but a Chinese syndicate wanted to buy the restaurant. Margo took them in and they ran the restaurant and split the bar with her. After having the band for two months we stopped using it; it was too expensive. When Margo sold her entire interest to the Chinese I took a job playing at Isbell's, a jazz club and restaurant, so I could support her.

She used to come in and sit at the bar every night. Estilita saw my picture in the paper and came by with some guy, and when she saw Margo at the bar she said, "She's too old for you." Margo was a few years older than I and had been married a couple of times, once to a scientist. When she got a big royalty check from one of his books she suggested we go to New York City where I could get more work.

We went and soon afterward I got a call from an agent who asked if I would like to take six men to a place in East St. Louis for three weeks. It was sort of an underworld hangout, a great big place. The owner was a tough guy but very nice to me; he had a wonderful respect for musicians. I took trumpeter Ruby Brath and pianist Paul Jordan. The other guys were from St. Louis. The job paid very well and everyone was very pleasant to us. About four o'clock in the morning the boss used to take me down to a place where you could get some pretty good food and drinks, where a lot of show people and restaurateurs hung out. One morning a blonde professional came over and threw her arms around me. The boss came over and snarled, "Get away from my saxophone player; he's different than us." Then he turned to me and said, "Buddy, if you want to get laid, I'll get you fixed up. Don't mess around with these broads."

We were there for three weeks when Margo called me and said that her mother had died and left her this tremendous amount of money. She wanted me to quit playing and go to Chile with her, which I did. We went to Viña del Mar and we had a beautiful apartment, right on the sea, and we had servants, which I didn't like. I could never be happy living like that, with all that money to burn.

I was terribly unhappy because I wasn't playing, I wasn't doing my thing. It seems to me that if you live off a woman she eventually comes to hate you for it. She resents it to no end. Margo resented my living off her, especially since our love affair had ended. So I said to myself, "Well, if ever I get back to New York, I don't care if I make fifteen dollars a week, I'm never going to live off another woman." I had done that several times in my career. When things had gone bad and I didn't want to work in some sawdust place I'd take off with some woman. It wasn't that I looked for the woman. The type of woman I've always loved, the elegant type, always seemed to have money and would always take me by the hand. I never went after a woman because she had money. It was just that type of woman I ended up with, and then, of course, we would fall out of love and I would be in trouble.

I had the dream that many men have about having a lot of money. Now finally I had it and could do anything I wanted and buy anything I wanted, yet I was terribly unhappy because it wasn't mine. So I said to myself, "When I get back to the States, if I can make fifteen dollars a week, at least I can hold my head up." We moved back to New York after ten months. The first job I had paid me only twenty-five dollars, but I didn't care, I was so glad to have it. I was hardly the only musician to have lived off a rich woman. I could name seven other tenor saxists who have done it. Jack Pettis, one of the original members of the New Orleans Rhythm Kings, was one. He married an heiress. Now I understand what Laurence Olivier meant when he told me one night that the tenor was very sexy.

"I Remember Rio"

When Margo and I came back from Chile we checked into a hotel and right away began looking for an apartment in the Village. I found an ad for a place on West Thirteenth Street between Fifth and Sixth avenues and went over. When I got there I found a lot of other people waiting to see it. The apartment, I discovered, was owned by Max Eastman, the famous writer and socialist. It was a lovely place. After we introduced ourselves I told Max, "I didn't realize you were the famous Max Eastman." He said, "Well, I didn't realize you were the famous Bud Freeman." We both laughed; then he said to the others, "Thank you very much for waiting, but this gentleman has taken the apartment."

Margo and I stayed there about six months, and during that time Eastman and I became friends. He and his wife took a summer home at Chilmark, on the Cape, but he came into town every so often. In 1950, six months after moving in, Margo left for Mexico and that was the last I ever saw of her. I left Eastman's apartment, which was quite expensive, and found a room at the Van Rensselaer Hotel for twenty-eight dollars a week.

Pee Wee Russell was then living in New York, and he started taking me around to the Cedar Bar & Grill in the Village, just north of Washington Square. The Cedar was strictly a rendezvous for artists, actors, musicians, playwrights, and newspapermen. Well-known painters, including Jackson Pollock, Stuart Davis, and Willem de Kooning, hung out there. Pee Wee was a good friend of Stuart and introduced me to him. I saw a lot of Stuart and the others. They were jazz fans. Stuart, in fact, used to paint while listening to jazz music, and all of them went out together on Friday nights to jazz clubs.

True, they spent a lot of time at the Cedar, but most of them were not heavy drinkers. De Kooning, in fact, was quite serious and seldom drank, but Pollack was alcoholic and sort of suicidal. I saw him at the Cedar the night he died. He was quite drunk. His painter friends pleaded with him not to get into his car, but he did and drove onto the highway and was killed.

There was another painter by the name of Mischa Resnikoff who hung out at the Cedar and who, like Pollock, painted in the famous drip style. I saw his works before I saw Pollock's and I'm not sure which man created this style. Years later, when I was playing with The World's Greatest Jazz Band, Walter Cronkite came up to me and said, "I understand you know a lot of painters. Do you know anything about this drip painting?" "I know Mischa Resnikoff," I said. "He's a friend of mine." Cronkite said, "I'd like to buy one of his paintings." I gave him Mischa's phone number and called Mischa and said, "For God's sake, don't give this thing away. Walter can afford to pay a good fee for it." But he sold one of them to Walter for $1,000 when he could have sold it for $5,000. Mischa's wife, a photographer for *Life* magazine, supported him. She took a photograph of Margo and me in Eastman's apartment for a well-known magazine.

During my stay at the Van Rensselaer I began running Friday and Saturday night jazz sessions in the hotel's dining room. Two former Gibson Girls who lived there used to come to these sessions; so did Stuart, Mischa, Phillip Hamburger, and John O'Hara. I held these for about fifteen weeks. They were always sold out but I only made forty dollars each session. Of course, I was doing other work. They were simply a labor of love. I had Joe Bushkin, Buck Clayton, Jonah Jones, Buster Bailey, Dave Bowman, George Wettling, Dick Cary, and others. I would try to give everybody a shot at it; it used to pay them thirty dollars. The chef was a black guy and he liked the fact that I was using black musicians, so he'd put out a big buffet for us.

Estilita and I got divorced in 1955. We had been separated when I went off to Chile with Margo, and I wouldn't have bothered to get a divorce had it not been for a stunning woman named Marie whom I met at one of the Van Rensselaer sessions. She was sitting there alone and the man who ran the bar introduced me to her. She was a little lady, blond and light-complexioned, and she always wore lovely hats and smoked with a cigarette holder. She was a journalist. After going together for several months she told me that she suffered from encephalitis, a kind of sleeping sickness she had contracted from a mosquito bite in the Everglades. She had a live-in secretary, not only to take dictation, but to be with her in case she passed out from the illness.

During the war Marie had written propaganda pamphlets that were dropped from planes over Germany. They said things like, "Are you enjoying your food?" "How's your house?" At that time the Americans and Russians were pillaging everything in Germany. Marie also spent a lot of time during the war visiting the wounded at Walter Reed Hospital in Washington. There was one man there whom she used to tease all the time, saying, "Are you going to go on gold-bricking for the rest of the war?" She found out later that he was Hap Arnold, a five-star general who was in command of the U.S. Army Air Corps.

While Marie and I were seeing each other I was going off to play clubs and concerts across the United States and Canada. For instance, Jimmy McPartland and I appeared at the Preview in Chicago for a month. I also played in Toronto several times and at New York clubs, too, including the Stuyvesant Casino and the Central Plaza. The Central Plaza had jazz sessions on weekends with fine musicians like Willie "The Lion" Smith, Coleman Hawkins, "Hot Lips" Page, Bobby Hackett, and Max Kaminsky. Whenever I was out of town I would call Marie every night and she'd say, "Hurry up and come back!" We were inseparable, really, and very much in love. We were together for about a year before she died from the encephalitis; she had been able to fight it off for about four years. Now I understand that if a child gets it the child dies immediately, but she had a horrible time. She'd fall asleep and burn herself with cigarettes. To make things worse, my father died at age seventy-nine just a few months before she did.

When Marie died I went into shock, then into a depression. Work did nothing to take my mind off my loss. One night, after playing a concert in Greenwich, Connecticut, I got back to Grand Central Station about midnight and took the one cab waiting outside. The driver was a black man somewhere in his forties and for some reason I decided to open up and tell him my troubles. I talked all the way downtown to my apartment in the Village. When we got there he turned off the meter and looked back at me and said, "Have you ever heard of Lao-tzu?" I said, "No," and he began telling me about Taoism and Zen Buddhism. "The reason you're unhappy," he said, "is because you're thinking about yourself and what you've been deprived of. If you understood the idea of Zen, that couldn't happen. If you understood Zen, your thoughts of your friend would be sweet and you would realize that she was very ill and that it was better for her to have died." He suggested that I read several books, the first of which, *The Way of Life According to Lao Tzu*, was Witter Bynner's "translation" of Lao-tzu's *Tao Te Ching*. From there I went on to read numerous works on Zen, including D. T. Suzuki's *Zen Buddhism* and Eugen Herrigel's *Zen and the Art of Archery*.

Herrigel, who was German, had gotten an appointment as a professor of philosophy at the University of Tokyo. He was deeply interested in mysticism and wanted to immerse himself in Zen, but not in an academic fashion. Instead, he wanted to experience the *unio mystica*. When Herrigel broached the matter to several Japanese he was told that Zen was difficult if not impossible for a European to penetrate. Finally, his acquaintances told him that the best way to approach Zen would be to study one of the arts traditionally associated with it. Herrigel, who was a rifleman, thought that archery best suited him and eventually persuaded a Zen master who was an archer to accept him as a pupil. One day, after a long period of study, he hit the bull's eye, and though he had hit it before, this time the master bowed and said, "Just then 'It' shot." "It" was the Way. The Way, as I understand it, means acting in a completely relaxed fashion. In the case of archery, hitting the bull's eye is not the point. A person might practice any art or craft all of his life without hitting the "bull's eye"; that is irrelevant.

The aim of Zen and Taoist practices lies in the attempt to lose one's self-centeredness, one's ego. Bynner's book has a wonderful line that sums it up: "If you never assume importance you never lose it." I found that attitude in a story told in another of the Eastern books. According to the story, Confucius and Lao-tzu were contemporaries, and when Confucius heard of Lao-tzu's great peace of mind, he searched all over for him. When he finally found the sage living in a cave Confucius asked him, "How can I attain the absolute peace of mind which you seem to have?" Lao-tzu replied, "Rid yourself of your haughty manner."

Another book tells of a distraught young woman who went to a Japanese psychiatrist, crying, "I just found out that I'm illegitimate." The psychiatrist looked at her and said, "What were you before you were illegitimate?"

Within a few months after reading these books I became happier and more relaxed than I'd ever been and was able to work harder than ever without tiring. My outlook became much more Eastern. I lost all sense of competition. Most Western artists are very competitive; competition is embedded in their culture. For example, when one jazz artist has to follow another artist who has just stopped the show, the first one thinks, How can I compete with that? How can I cut that? That was my attitude before I got into Zen. After I got into it I'd think, Why should I make myself miserable thinking about how I'm going to cut another player?

After I realized the stupidity of competition I found myself at a concert, waiting backstage to follow a tenor saxist who was jumping up and down, doing cartwheels, anything he could do to get the audience excited. They could have gone to the circus and had a better time, but he got a big hand. Instead of worrying about how I could get a bigger reaction from the audience I thought, There's nothing I can do about that, and I went out and played a ballad and got a great response.

If a man is really into his music he projects his concentration to the audience and they like it. If he talks to them, so much the better. He can't go on stage and turn his back on them. I'm very much for showmanship — I usually tell anecdotes at concerts — but a musician's showmanship is not as important as his involvement in the music. Zen artists are too involved in the creation of their work to think about its effect on others. Musicians, for example, do their best work when their spirits flow freely. That freedom of spirit can come to them when they play all night long. They can go up on the stand feeling ill and go off feeling marvelous and not be able to explain why.

Zen and Taoism cultivate freedom of spirit, which should be in everything we do. That's why I never practiced the kind of meditation that demands that the meditator fold his legs into pretzels for hours on end. That's a strain. People who do that are hoping for peace of mind, but real peace comes through freedom of spirit. Real meditation does not have any strict rules.

After two years of studying Zen I got away from it. It wasn't that I'd lost interest, I just started to read other things. But as a result of my reading books on Zen I seemed to get a lot more joy out of all the arts and seemed to know what was nonsense and what wasn't. My taste seemed to improve.

Three months after Marie's death I met a brilliant child therapist named Faye, whom I married in Greenwich Village. In 1962 George Wein invited us to a party at his home, where I met Gerald Lascelles, Queen Elizabeth II's cousin. Gerald spent the entire evening talking to me. A mob of writers were trying to get near him but he paid them no attention. He said, "Would you like to come over for a concert in Manchester, England?" He and Lord Montagu were organizing the first international British jazz festival. I accepted. It was my first European date, a concert with Dizzy Gillespie and Buck Clayton. Each of us was there a week, fronting a different band. The people gave us a tremendous ovation. Now bear in mind that the festival was sold out and there were thousands of people there. I turned around to see who they were applauding. I couldn't believe it was for us because we had never got that kind of ovation in the United States. People in Europe know every record you've made. They come backstage and say, "Hey, you didn't play it that way on the record." It was a great thrill, and on the strength of that trip I decided that I would eventually like to live in Europe.

In the fall of 1963 I learned rather painfully just how important playing was to me. Al Seidel and I were stuck in bumper-to-bumper traffic on New York's Queensborough Bridge, coming back from the racetrack. Once we started moving again and had managed to speed up to about forty miles per hour when a panel truck coming from the opposite direction shot out in front of us. There was no way we could avoid hitting it. Al slammed on the brakes, grabbed the wheel, and we swerved sideways into the truck. He was buffered by the wheel, but I was hurled forward into the dashboard and hit the side of my chest. When the initial shock passed I felt a severe pain. I could barely breathe and I felt that something was broken.

Al was all right, just a bit shaken. I got out of the car and flagged down a cab, jumped in, and rode to my apartment on Ninety-sixth Street, between Park and Madison avenues. Faye was downstairs in her office; her two aunts, who were visiting us, were upstairs. I had them pour me a glass of vodka as Faye called her doctor. He came over, gave me a shot, and ordered an ambulance, which took me to a hospital in

Harlem. X-rays showed that I had multiple fractures of the right rib cage. I had been wearing a thick corduroy coat and had my wallet in my right breast pocket, which I think may have lessened the impact. The bone specialist who was tending me wanted to give me drugs but I said, "No, I'd rather have the pain." I was afraid I might become an addict.

Lots of people in the hospital knew of me, and I almost always had visitors, especially after my brother, Arny, who was living in New York, brought me a television set so I could watch the World Series. Plenty of interns took their breaks in my room. Al came by. He and his wife were about to go to Europe on a vacation and he apologized for leaving, but I said, "My God, you can't do any good here." Jason Robards, whom I had known from the jazz sessions at the Van Rensselaer, came to visit once.

I was released after fifteen days, but the pain was so severe for six or seven weeks afterward that I had to practice different ways of getting in and out of bed. Once a week I would return to the bone specialist, but other than X-rays at the hospital and his weekly exams, I had no medical treatment. I did not play for seven months. Perhaps I could have begun sooner, but I was afraid of hurting myself. I spent the time reading, seeing plays and films, and walking.

During my convalescence Faye suggested that I go into psychotherapy. "Why don't you try it?" she said. "You might get something out of it." I thought, What harm can it do me? and I agreed to it, even though I was not unhappy. The therapist was wonderful, but there were still days when I would say, "I never want to see that son of a bitch again." Those were days when he'd say anything to make me angry and open up, things like, "Jesus Christ, I don't even know who you are!" Other days I'd leave his office kicking stones and cans, I'd be so happy.

Despite the alternating highs and lows I stayed with it for a couple of years. It was a wonderful experience. If you get the right doctor and have the courage to open up and talk about yourself honestly, then psychotherapy can do wonders. If the doctor is not a phony, the doctor can become the patient and the patient, the doctor—at least that was my experience. There were a few times when I felt like the doctor, as though I were trying to teach him a few things. I remember the day he said we could discontinue our sessions. I was somewhat shocked and hurt and said I wanted to stay in therapy, but he said, "You're an artist. You're supposed to be a little crazy. You don't need to continue with this." He was a hell of a guy.

In the meantime I had contacted a very sharp lawyer who made his living going after insurance companies, and after eighteen months he settled out of court with the truck driver's insurer. I was quite pleased with the settlement but wouldn't want to repeat the accident, even for that kind of money.

The first date I had after my recovery came from Art Hodes, a pianist I had known in the twenties. Art had a television show in Chicago and invited me to play on it. Believe me, I was delighted; getting back to the horn was one of the happiest events in my life.

I started taking more and more European bookings and went once with a Condon all-star group to Japan, where we received a gala reception. After the plane taxied up to the gate, airport attendants rolled out a red carpet and Eddie came staggering out of the airplane door and down the stairs. There was a committee to receive this honored guest, among them a woman with a large bouquet of flowers who walked very smartly up the carpet to him. Eddie's hat was tipped over his head, his hair had fallen over his face, his shirttail was sticking over his trousers. He was missing a shoe. Without changing her expression this woman walked up to him, gave him the flowers, and with a very military about-face walked off. Dick Cary and I were on the side laughing.

Then, to the amazement of the Japanese, Eddie played the first concert sober. They were terribly disappointed because their papers had said that he was on a big drunk. We were there for several days, and at the end of our stay Eddie broke down and got smashed in the lobby of the Imperial Hotel. This was a very elegant place, designed by Frank Lloyd Wright, and there Eddie was without a jacket or tie, stopping everybody to talk and tell stories. The Japanese were tee-heeing; they thought he was a stitch.

Eddie must have had an incredible constitution because he was drunk all of his life. He was in the hospital several times for his alcoholism, but I think he drank right to the end. I was on the road when he died in 1974; it was something we expected because he was in the hospital and was going through a tremendous amount of pain. I had played with him in a concert shortly before he went into the hospital and he had lost a lot of weight. He had fought off death many times—he had had serious pancreas infections—but he was certainly not frightened of dying. He had been warned many times by his doctors to give up drinking, but he didn't. He never gave death a thought.

It was during these tours that I realized it would be best for Faye and me to break up. She knew everything about children and nothing about men. I don't mean to defend myself, because I might not have been the best husband in the world, but we just didn't get along and I had to leave. In fact, we're still estranged; I haven't seen her in fifteen years. We lived together from 1958 to 1963. In the five years that followed I spent most of my time on the Continent, and whenever work was slow I'd come back for a month or so and stay with Arny in California. Sometimes he would visit me in London. He was making a good living as an actor. In the thirties he had acted in a Chicago repertory company with Studs Terkel. Studs, of course, went on to become a Pulitzer Prize–winning writer; Arny remained an actor. He had had parts in Broadway hits with Alfred Lunt and Lynn Fontanne, with Jason Robards and others. He was always in hits, and always as a supporting actor.

About 1969 a man by the name of Dick Gibson began hiring jazz musicians to play for private parties in various western towns. The musicians thought Gibson was paying for these parties, but it turned out that he was being backed by a millionaire. Gibson had a huge mailing list and sent out invitations to other millionaires around the country, who paid quite a sum to come to these black-tie affairs. These parties, or festivals, ran about three days. Once a year Gibson would throw one at Denver's Elitch Gardens, an elegant amusement park, and another in Odessa, Texas, a small oil town. He had them in Aspen and elsewhere. Gibson had chosen the musicians himself, and the nucleus included Bob Haggart, Yank Lawson, Billy Butterfield, and me.

During the time I was playing the Gibson sessions Pee Wee Russell took up painting. It wasn't his idea; his wife, Mary, suggested it to him because he wasn't finding much work. She went out and bought him some paint, brushes, and canvasses. Pee Wee, who wasn't drinking very much then, took to it like a duck to water. During his years of heavy drinking he must have been seeing things with a third eye, because these paintings, which showed the influence of Stuart Davis and Joan Míro, were remarkable. Quite a few people thought so. I sold three of them for him.

In fact, Pee Wee had made enough of a name for himself that the Australian ambassador invited him to show his work in Washington, D.C., along with several Australian and New Zealand painters. The opening was going to be a black-tie affair and Mary told me that Pee Wee refused to go. The possibility that his paintings might become better known excited me and I called him to urge him to go. He declined, saying that he didn't have a black tie. Sadly, Pee Wee didn't think of himself as a painter.

Gibson's sessions, meanwhile, were proving so successful that he decided we could have a very commercial ten-piece band. We had been playing these parties with nine musicians; Gibson added a banjo player and sold the band to a place called the Riverboat in New York City. He called us The World's Greatest Jazz Band. Originally, we had Yank Lawson and Billy Butterfield on trumpet, Bob Haggart on bass, Ralph Sutton on piano, Morey Feld on drums, Vic Dickenson and Lou McGarrity on trombone, Clancy Hayes on banjo, Bob Wilber on clarinet and soprano sax, and me on tenor. Eventually we cut the band down to seven men and hired Gus Johnson to replace Marty when Marty died. Bob Haggart made some beautiful arrangements of all the then-popular composers, such as Burt Bacharach, Jimmy Webb, and the Beatles; I loved these much more than the big band arrangements of the thirties. Our job at the Riverboat was a great success. A few months later we moved to the Downbeat Room. After that Gibson got us in the Roosevelt Hotel. It was in the Roosevelt Grill that Guy Lombardo had played years before. By the time we went in nothing had happened in the room in about thirty years. We had a fantastic time for about a year and did a marvelous business.

We played the finest clubs in the country. We traveled an awful lot. For one month we did a string of one-nighters that took us from New York to San Francisco. We went to Europe two or three times and we played in Brazil, Hawaii, and Alaska. What a delight it was to be in Alaska wearing civilian clothes. When we went to Rio de Janeiro I took the guys to the old room I had played in back in 1947, and it brought back memories of the Brazilians dancing the samba to everything we played.

It surprised us to discover that we were much better known in Europe than in the United States. We had just finished playing a concert in Edinburgh, Scotland, and we flew the next day to Omaha, Nebraska, where we were booked to play at a country club. They had never before had a famous jazz band play for their dances; they had always had so-called society music, so this was a big event for them. A local newspaper sent one of its reporters to do a piece on the band, and Yank and Bob asked me to take the interview. The journalist was a lady somewhere in her seventies. She said, "I'm afraid I don't know very much about jazz." I said, "Don't worry, not many people do." Bob Haggart was standing nearby and she said, "Who's that?" I said, "That's Bob Haggart, one of the world's greatest bass players, composers, and arrangers." She had never heard of him. Billy Butterfield was also standing nearby having a drink and she said, "Who's that?" I said, "That's Billy Butterfield, one of the world's best ballad players." She had never heard of him either. Then she said, "And what's your name?" and I said, "Benny Goodman." She said, "Oh, I thought you were dead."

It was strange working in a band financed by a millionaire. It was sort of a plaything for him, and that was why we didn't compete with any of the big bands. If we worked a room for some shady character and he didn't pay us, we still got paid. If we didn't have work, Gibson would have a party and hire us. Everybody was happy because it was a labor-of-love band. I don't think we worked as much as six months a year. We could have made it in a very big way if it had been a hungry band, if it had been in the competitive swim of the music business and had done things bands have to do to make it. Many people who knew the business said the same thing. But we worked only when we liked because we had financing. We also had our own label, which wasn't a good idea. A musician has to have a top label that knows how to operate in the competitive recording business. We didn't.

I guess that Bob and Yank hardly work at all now. They're both very solvent and have beautiful homes and work only when it pleases them, but I'm glad that I left when I did, though I must say that I was very happy in the band. We had a lot of nice guys in it. And I always liked Bob and Yank.

In 1974 we went to Holland where we played concerts in Rotterdam and Amsterdam. Just before we boarded the plane to go back to London a little impressario came over and offered me a lot of money to play forty-five minutes at the Breide Festival. I accepted, and when my present agent in England, Robert Masters, heard it he said, "What the hell is going on? That's fantastic." He didn't know we were well known individually. In fact, we couldn't believe how well known we were. We never knew that because when you're in a band of all-stars you're just one soloist in a band of soloists.

Masters and a fellow by the name of Kennedy had the Kennedy-Masters Agency and they had been bringing bands overseas, paying large salaries and astronomically high travel expenses and losing a lot of money when the bands didn't sell out every night. I told Masters, "I'd like to stay over here and become a soloist. I'd like to have lunch with you one day and tell you what the solo field is all about." He didn't know that it existed, but he had marvelous contacts and got on the phone and everybody he called wanted me.

CHAPTER | N I N E

"After Awhile"

Thereafter I lived in London for six years. I had a marvelous time meeting people and going to the theater, but I worked terribly hard playing one-nighters and lived rather miserably in airports and railroad stations. That's why I gave it all up in 1980. There were, after all, just so many jobs I could do in London. Most of the work was on the Continent or in Ireland or on the Isle of Man. Sometimes I left London for an extensive tour of the Continent; sometimes I left to go to one country for a few days. In one case I was away for six and a half hours. Robert Masters, my agent, called me one day at 4 P.M. and asked if I could catch a 7:30 P.M. flight to Hanover, Germany, to play for eighteen minutes. I was to go on at 11 P.M. that night. I went, played the concert, and when I got off the stage a man said there was a car waiting to take me to the airport. He gave me an envelope with my pay in it and I found myself back in London at 2 A.M.

I think the dream of every jazz soloist is to work in the concert field, and that's why so many try to go to Europe, where they're treated like gods. The jazz musician is better paid at festivals than he is at clubs, and he feels he's more of an artist. In the concert field you do one or two shows and have some sort of decent life, not like the old days when we worked long hours in clubs and played eight or nine shows a day in theaters.

You burn yourself out working clubs. The people are noisy and drunk; they wear paper hats and they smoke. You walk out of there at the end of the evening and you've blown all the blood out of your body. Your clothes smell and your eyes and throat burn. A musician who plays clubs incessantly gets to boozing and into all kinds of habits that ordinarily he wouldn't have. He becomes sort of musically lethargic because he falls into the very easy trap of playing the same ideas all the time. If an artist goes into a jazz club and doesn't do a good business, the owners won't even talk to him. There are many things that could happen to turn business bad—poor weather or the club itself. The people who might have tremendous respect for an artist might not like the kind of place it is.

As for big band work, it's no different from working in a factory. You can't love music when you have to play it. Jazz is a luxurious music. You can't play it all the time and knock your fucking brains out. You've got to play it when you feel you're going to do something with it and create something. I've watched men in symphonies and big bands be insulted by conductors who were egomaniacal bastards. I've watched them worry themselves sick, afraid they were going to lose their jobs. Between clubs and big bands we had a hard time in the old days. This is why older jazz musicians today prefer to play concerts, and as a result we play better—those who cared enough to stay around. In a concert you go out and do your whole thing in one or two sets. You try more, you play better. In a jazz festival the people seem to be playing the music.

Playing is marvelous if the conditions are right. There's a feeling, something that comes over you, when people identify and love what you're doing. If I do play a club date now, I always have a group do three or four numbers before they introduce me, the way we do at concerts. It's a marvelous feeling; it's the greatest ego trip in the world. This is what we jazz soloists have been waiting for all of our lives. Nothing like the days when we had to play for some monstrous bandleader, someone who could insult you, say anything he felt. You were at the mercy of his whim, but now it's all changed. You're the boss.

Musicians, as young kids, think it's so romantic to play. They have no idea what a man goes through playing for sixty years. When I was young and very naive I used to think that actors and musicians were the luckiest people in the world. I thought they lived such romantic lives. Little did I know that the musician's life was one of the most difficult I could have chosen—playing one-nighters, riding in broken-down cars, eating bad food. Now, for the first time in my life, I can say to myself, Well, if I don't like the date I won't play it. All the jazz musician is asking is to be allowed to play his little saxophone, his little trombone or cornet, and be paid enough to have some sort of dignified life. God knows, he should be paid much more than he is because of the power of the music, therapeutically speaking.

It's a shame that so many famous American soloists have gone to Europe to make a living, but they must. An American jazz musician has got to play some terrible jobs to make a living. Perhaps that will all change. Perhaps America will again be "the" place for jazz because of its festivals, which are growing. Jazz isn't flourishing in clubs, in America or anywhere. Jazz clubs are a thing of the past, but the jazz business is bigger than ever and growing, thanks to festivals. Wherever festivals open, they sell out. People don't like hearing jazz at a nightclub anymore. They've got their records and they've got their festivals, where they can hear hundreds of the finest names in the world.

While Europe does have a large number of festivals, jazz musicians in England and on the Continent don't support themselves by working in festivals, clubs, or concert halls. The work is in pubs, which are wonderful places. Most British pubs are in small villages and are the hub of village social life. They're comfortable places, with large fireplaces, and usually they can seat quite a few patrons. People will go to one pub all their lives, and their children will go to the same one too. They're not expensive outside of jazz nights; any working person can go to one and have a few beers without paying very much.

Musicians play in pubs through arrangements made between the local jazz society and the local pub owner. Because these societies have the money to pay astronomical fees, all the great American soloists live in Europe. It is incredible that America does not have the societies that Europe has. In Germany there are 200 of them; in Holland there must be 40 or 50; in the U.K. about 135; in Italy about 30; in Switzerland about 25. There aren't many in France, but they're coming back. The audiences, especially in England and Germany, are great beer drinkers and are marvelous. To an English or European jazz fan there's no celebrity as great as a jazz musician. They are true lovers of that kind of music.

I lived in London for six years, so it was easy to get me; these societies didn't have to pay my fare across the Atlantic. I worked around something like a hundred little broken-down towns in the United Kingdom, each of which had a pub that featured American soloists who would play with the local group. Sometimes I played with a six-piece band but most often with a rhythm section. In many cases these jazz societies had some rich members, and in order to put the local group on the map they'd ask me to make an album, which was very expensive. In the six years I was there I made some forty-seven albums, nine of them in Holland.

Perhaps the most important thing that happened to me in Europe happened my first year there. I was on a two-week tour of Germany, Switzerland, Scotland, and Italy and during that time made a recording in Italy. Something happened during that session. I had chosen some ballads and while playing them found myself falling in love with a simpler way of playing. People love melodic line, and it took me about forty years of playing to discover that, and to discover it for myself. The great jazz musicians all played melodic line. Louis had a great regard for it; Bix had an even greater regard. It was always in my mind to play simply, but I was too wild to do it. I was like a young player: I wanted to make an impression. Now I don't have to.

After recording for forty years I finally came to realize that no one is ever going to give you an honest royalty so you have to get a lot of money in advance for doing an album. I started to do that in Europe. Producers would say, "Well, what do you want for an album? Do you want a royalty deal or do you want a flat fee?" I would say, "I want a flat fee," and I would charge them about $2,500. The producers might be very honorable, but somehow or other when it came time to pay royalties they all seemed to put them into their own pockets.

The British have been supporting jazz music for some seventy years. I remember that during the Second World War there were many majors and colonels in the British service who were jazz fans. I didn't know any officers in the American forces who knew anything about jazz or had the British regard for it. But I met many people from the small towns in the U.K. who told me that under fire they would have their little wireless sets on, listening to jazz programs such as were broadcast on the "Voice of America." To this very day the British have supported jazz. By the way, most of the popular jazz in Europe is danceable; it's swing-era music. They don't have big swing bands there, but they have many small bands with soloists who play a swing style, the Lester Young style, the Coleman Hawkins style, the Ben Webster style.

As I mentioned earlier, I had come to England at the invitation of

Gerald Lascelles, the Queen's cousin. Gerald was an amateur pianist and a jazz fan. His uncle, the Duke of Windsor, who was King Edward VIII for a short time, was also a jazz fan and was the man who used to give Dave Tough a tip so he could play Dave's drums all night. Gerald, though, was kind of stuffy. He'd call me up and in his Oxonian accent say, "Freeman, old chap, how about lunch in Mayfair?" He'd say it in this very standoffish tone, which was typical of him. He was always standoffish and never discussed personal matters. He had a fear that someone might get inside of him, but I think he was probably friendlier with me than with other Americans. He certainly liked my playing and heard me whenever I played in London.

He was a big, robust fellow with a bland face and a tremendous appetite, which was my misfortune because whenever we went out I always seemed to pick up the tab. One day I said, "Gerald, don't you ever have any fucking money?" He said, "Oh, no, we don't carry any." I said, "What if I didn't carry any? Then we'd really be in a jam, wouldn't we? We'd have to wash dishes." He was sort of nonplussed by that. I handed him the bill and said, "You take this and give it to your cousin, the Queen, with my compliments." He smiled and signed it. I'd be damned if I was going to pay for another meal.

When Edward VIII abdicated he left Fort Belvedere to Gerald, or so we thought. Gerald lived there and gave a lot of parties, but it actually belonged to the Crown. When the Crown sold it to some Arabs for a tremendous amount of money, Gerald left his wife, who was an actress and a lovely woman, and moved into town with a young gal. How he supports her, I don't know. I suppose he gets his living expenses from the Crown.

Whenever I was in London I spent much of my time at the Audley Arms, a pub in Grovernor Square, near the American embassy. The food was excellent and the people interesting. It wasn't uncommon to see a guy in a silk hat talking to a sailor. The place served a Danish beer, the strongest beer I've ever tasted. Two of those and I would be ready to roll on the floor.

I belonged to a little roulette club called the Connoisseur. I was playing roulette one night when Peter Boizot, one of the owners, came up and asked, "Are you Bud Freeman?" When I said I was he said, "I own twenty places called the Pizza Express and I wondered if you'd like to start a jazz policy at one of them." This particular restaurant could hold about fifty-five or sixty people, and because I started the jazz sessions there, Peter named one of the pizzas after me. It cost three pounds forty and it's still on the menu. The jazz concerts there are still a big success. Virtually every big name in the solo field has played there.

There was always something to do in London. When I wasn't working I was going to the wonderful British theater or having a drink with friends. I have very fond memories of times spent with a pianist named Lenny Felix, who was killed in a car accident, and with Max Jones, a very bright, very interesting writer who has done more for jazz in Europe than any other writer. I knew quite a few people in government, too, and was invited to the House of Commons for a champagne brunch once a month. Peter arranged for that. I knew people all over the U.K., so I often had friends to stay with when I toured.

Since I had been a lifelong Anglophile, it was with some pleasure that I bought a British warm overcoat in 1963. I had always wanted one. In those days it was a coat worn just by the British military—colonels, generals, and majors. I was wearing it one day, walking to Regent Street, when a young woman came up and said, "Major, can you direct me to Pickadillam?" "Pickadillam" is the British upper-crust pronunciation for Piccadilly. Without batting an eyelash I said, "Yes, my deah, up to the tawp, to the right, and theah you ah." She said, "Thank you ver, ver much," and I said, "Nawt-a-tall," and sauntered off in my coat.

I was backstage at the opera house in Amsterdam during a concert when Robert Masters said that a lady by the name of Penny Tyler, who was president of the Jazz Institute of Chicago, had called to ask if I could play a concert in Chicago at Grant Park. I said I'd love to. I had no idea that I was going to stay in the States.

After six years in London I had become rather British. Most of us, after all, pick up the habits of the people we live with, and I did have a lot of dear friends in England. When I came back everybody told me I had a British accent. After I was introduced to the huge audience at the Jazz Institute festival I came forward and in my Oxonian accent said, "Ladies and gentlemen, what a dee-*light* to be home in Chicago." A drunk yelled out, "Fer Chrissake, Freeman, you're in Chicago, speak like an American." I put my hand to the side of my mouth and called back, "Okay, bub."

Penny Tyler and her friend, guitarist John De Fauw, had found me an apartment in a residential hotel for the week of the festival, and in that short time I rediscovered Chicago. I wasn't sure that I would stay in the States, but I was delighted with my hometown. It was cosmopolitan and livable, and I decided to stay for a while. The hotel manager said that if I went on a European tour I would always have a room to come back to. I did return to Europe two or three times after the Jazz Institute festival but decided I'd had enough of the hard work and wanted a rest. I decided to stay in Chicago.

Now, hardly a month goes by that I don't receive three or four invitations to play U.S. or European festivals. Some of the U.S. offers I accept, but not the European ones, though I have been tempted. When an impressario tries to book me for a European date, I thank him politely but explain that I've lived out of airports and train stations long enough. Sometimes they don't understand that a man can have just so much of that life, that it is exhausting to travel several thousand miles to play a concert, to pack the next day and travel some more, to play another concert, to travel again, to play another concert. A year ago a German impressario called me from Hamburg and asked if I would play a series of German festivals. When I told him that I didn't care for the grinding schedule he'd offered, he said, "But Herr Freeman, we have excellent hospitals in Germany."

I think audiences come to hear older musicians like me just to see if we can pick up a horn without falling over. That's why impressarios don't hang up on me when I tell them I only play short sets. They probably know I'm senile, too, that when I start playing I forget about time. I remember two years ago I was playing a benefit in a Chicago club called Andy's, co-owned by Penny Tyler. I was supposed to play for only twenty minutes but when I got off I was told that I had been up there for an hour. That says something for the power and the joy of this music.

That is why I continue playing, why I still travel to festivals. During 1987–88 I played festivals in New York, Wisconsin, Arizona, Illinois, Pennsylvania, and California, plus half a dozen dates in the city where Louis and King Oliver discovered a beat that will be with us forever, the city where Bix and Bessie Smith, Jimmie Noone, Earl Hines, and a score of other greats developed a music that came from the spirit of the blacks, the city where it all started for me and where I live again. Chicago.

Selected Discography

This annotated discography is limited to a few of my recording dates and generally to a few of the tunes cut at any one session. Since a fair number of the songs listed are originals, I think it's worth recounting how they came about.

For years on end jazz musicians have been playing very creative choruses on given songs. Take any popular tune. A jazz musician would come along and improvise a beautiful chorus, which would become another song. Publishers would pick these songs up and give them another name and the man who created them got nothing. The jazz musician was lucky if he ended up with his name on it. If the jazz musicians of the twenties and thirties had been business people and had known about contracts, we would be rich men today.

There was a tune that I used to play, and on that tune I had an improvised chorus that became another song. Tommy Dorsey said, "Bud, don't give those choruses away to publishers. They're going to steal them. You improved the chorus, so make another song out of it. Give it a title and have it published under your own name." So when Tommy advised me about that, I took all of my improvised choruses on given themes and gave them different titles. Nobody's stealing anything by doing that. Improvised composition on the original theme becomes a better piece of music in most cases. Besides, where did the composers get their ideas anyway?

Even when I did give the tune a name and published it I ended up with practically nothing. I must have recorded sixty or seventy originals in the sixty years I've been recording. I don't receive all of the royalties I should, but somebody's getting them. That's my own fault. I didn't do anything about it, as in the case where I recorded some originals on the early Commodore Records. Little did

I dream that those things were going to become collector's items. The last Bud Freeman trio date with George Wettling and Jess Stacy was reissued by Commodore about ten years ago and was a tremendous hit; in fact, it's a very big seller in Europe today. But I got nothing out of them outside of the thirty-dollar fee for each session. Now there's something wrong with that. But I was stupid. I didn't do anything about a contract; I didn't do anything about a royalty deal. I just went in and recorded those things. It was a labor of love and that was the end of it. So you know who got the money. Suppose I did want to make a case of it, what could I get? Even if I won, by the time I got through paying the lawyers I wouldn't have anything. I have no one to blame but myself.

A Guide to Codes

The number to the left of each song title indicates the recording's master number; the number to the right indicates the record number of the first issue; the letters preceeding the record number indicate the label on which it was issued. I am indebted to Brian Rust's *Jazz Records, 1897–1942* (4th ed.) for refreshing my memory on personnel and for providing dates plus master and record numbers.

Record Labels
Aff = Affinity (American); B1 = Bluebird (American); Br = Brunswick (American); Col = Columbia (American); Com = Commodore (American); Dec = Decca (American); Od = Odeon (English); OK = OKeh (American); Par = Parlophone (English); UA = United Artists (American); Vic = Victor (American)

Instruments
tp = trumpet; c = cornet; tb = trombone; vtb = valve trombone; cl = clarinet; as = alto sax; ts = tenor sax; p = piano; g = guitar; bj = banjo; sb = string bass; bb = brass bass; d = drums; v = vocalist; a = arranger

MCKENZIE & CONDON'S CHICAGOANS
Jimmy McPartland, c; Frank Teschemacher, cl; Bud Freeman, ts; Joe Sullivan, p; Eddie Condon, bj; Jim Lannigan, sb & bb; Gene Krupa, d
Chicago, Dec. 8, 1927

82030-A	Sugar	OK 41011
82031-B	China Boy	OK 41011

Chicago, Dec. 16, 1927

82082-B	Nobody's Sweetheart	OK 40971
82083-A	Liza	OK 40971

BUD FREEMAN AND HIS ORCHESTRA

Johnny Mandel, tp; Floyd O'Brien, tb; Bud Jacobson, cl; Bud Freeman, ts; Dave North, p; Herman Foster, bj; John Mueller, sb; Gene Krupa, d; Red McKenzie, v

Chicago, Dec. 3, 1928

| 402151-C | Craze-O-logy | OK 41168 |
| 402152-B-C | Can't Help Lovin' Dat Man | OK 41168 |

Claude Thornhill and Artie Shaw grew up together and listened to these sides as young men. They used to play them over and over because it was such an unusual style of tenor. Claude thought that was a very powerful influence on Shaw's later playing. At the time, everybody was trying to play like Coleman Hawkins.

EDDIE CONDON AND HIS ORCHESTRA

Max Kaminsky, tp; Floyd O'Brien, tb; Pee Wee Russell, cl; Bud Freeman, ts; Alex Hill, p; Eddie Condon, bj; Artie Bernstein, sb; Sid Catlett, d

New York, Oct. 21, 1933

| B-14193-A | The Eel | Br | 02006 |

personnel: same as above except Joe Sullivan replaced Alex Hill

New York, Nov. 17, 1933

| B-14193-C | The Eel | Br 6743 |

RAY NOBLE AND HIS ORCHESTRA

Pee Wee Erwin & Charlie Spivak, tp; Glenn Miller, tb & a; Will Bradley, tb; Johnny Mince & Mike Doty or Jim Cannon & Milt Yaner, cl & as; Bud Freeman, ts; Claude Thornhill, p; George Van Eps, g; Delmar Kaplar, sb; Bill Harty, d; Al Bowlly & The Freshman, v

New York, Oct. 9, 1935

| 95191-1 | Dinah | Vic 25223 |

"Dinah" started out as a ballad and went into double time. Someone—I think it was Lester Young—said that my solo was the first example of so-called cool playing. I played the tune with a little sound that Lester would later make famous.

BUD FREEMAN AND HIS WINDY CITY FIVE

Bunny Berigan, tp; Bud Freeman, cl; Claude Thornhill, p; Eddie Condon, g; Grachan Mancur, sb; Cozy Cole, d

New York, Dec. 4, 1935

| 60191-A | The Buzzard | Par R-2210 |
| 60191-B | The Buzzard | Dec 18112 |

I was playing with Ray Noble then and asked Claude to join me for this. He said, "I'm not a jazz musician," but I said, "I want you on the date." Condon told John Hammond, who was running the date, that I was very good on clarinet, so that's why I played it on "The Buzzard," which is an original. We recorded this for English Decca–Parlophone. This session wasn't released in the States until after the war.

BUD FREEMAN TRIO
Bud Freeman, ts; Jess Stacy, p; George Wettling, d
New York, Jan. 17, 1938

22311-1	You Took Advantage of Me	Com 501
22312-1	Three's No Crowd	Com 501
22313-1	I Got Rhythm	Com 502

New York, Apr. 13, 1938

22719-2	Keep Smilin' at Trouble	Com 503
22720-1	At Sundown	Com 503
22721-1	My Honey's Lovin' Arms	Com 504
22722-2	I Don't Believe It	Com 504

Of all of my Commodore sides, I am happiest with this April 13 session.

New York, Nov. 30, 1938

75952-A	Three Little Words	Com 514
75958-A	Swingin' without Mezz	Com 514
75959-A	The Blue Room	Com 513
75960-A	Exactly Like You	Com 513

"Swingin' without Mezz" and "I Don't Believe It" were originals. I was the leader and got only thirty dollars for the session. "Swingin' without Mezz" got its title because he had recorded "Swingin' with Mezz."

BUD FREEMAN AND HIS GANG
Bobby Hackett, c; Dave Mathews, as; Bud Freeman, ts; Pee Wee Russell, cl; Jess Stacy, p; Eddie Condon, g; Artie Shapiro, sb; Dave Tough or Marty Marsala, d
New York, July 12, 1938

23233-1	Tappin' the Commodore Till	Com 508
23235-1	Life Spears a Jitterbug	Com 507

"Tappin' the Commodore Till" was an original. So was "Life Spears a Jitterbug," which got its title from the special jazz issue that *Life* magazine put together that year.

TOMMY DORSEY AND HIS ORCHESTRA
> Pee Wee Erwin, Joe Bauer, Andy Ferretti, tp; Tommy Dorsey, Les Jenkins, Red Bone, tb; Johnny Mince & Mike Doty, cl & as; Bud Freeman, ts; Howard Smith, p; Carmen Mastren, g & a; Gene Traxer, sb; Dave Tough, d; Edythe Wright & Jack Leonard, v

New York, Apr. 15, 1937

> 011357-1   Smoke Gets in Your Eyes   Vic 25657
> personnel: same as above except Walter Mercurio replaced Red Bone; Mike Doty not on line-up; Fred Stulce (as) and Skeets Herfurt (as) added

New York, July 20, 1937

> 07810-1   Stop, Look and Listen!   Vic 36207

Of all the recordings I did with Tommy I'm happiest with "Stop, Look and Listen!" and "Smoke Gets in Your Eyes." In my chorus on "Stop, Look and Listen!" I used a sort of anticipated thing, a stop beat. It was a dance beat that I had seen black guys do. I was told that Lester Young was influenced by it. Lester's first album after he left Count Basie had it. There was also a phrase in "Smoke Gets in Your Eyes" that I made by tying two phrases together. Tunes were made out of that. Alex Stordhal and Paul Weston were arrangers for Dorsey then, and they brought it up to me. They said, "There's another phrase they'll be using."

Incidentally, there were very few critics who understood what I was doing when I was playing for Dorsey. Some absolutely hated my thing, and one went so far as to say, "I wish somebody would stuff a mouthpiece down his throat." Well, I got a call from an agent who said, "Jeez, Freeman, you're getting a lot of bad write-ups. You want to go to work for the office?" In other words, "You want to work? You'll do good business now."

EDDIE CONDON AND HIS WINDY CITY SEVEN
> Bobby Hackett, c; George Brunis, tb; Pee Wee Russell, cl; Bud Freeman, ts; Jess Stacy, p; Eddie Condon, g; Artie Shapiro, sb; George Wettling, d

New York, Jan. 17, 1938

> 22307-1   Beat to the Socks   Com 502
> 22308-1   Carnegie Drag   Com 1500
> 22309-1   Carnegie Jump   Com 1500

I was playing with Benny Goodman at the Waldorf-Astoria when we recorded these. All three tunes are originals, but I don't know where the titles came from. I do know that I get royalty checks on them once in awhile.

New York, Apr. 30, 1938

> 22833-1   Serenade to a Shylock   Com 1501

personnel: same as above except Jack Teagarden replaced George Brunis

| 22832-2 | Diane | Com 505 |

"Serenade to a Shylock" is also an original. The most outstanding thing on that session was Teagarden's solo on "Diane."

EDDIE CONDON AND HIS BAND

Bobby Hackett, c; Vernon Brown, tb; Pee Wee Russell, cl; Bud Freeman, ts; Joe Bushkin, p; Eddie Condon, g; Artie Shapiro, sb; Lionel Hampton, d
New York, Nov. 12, 1938

| 23706-1 | Sunday | Com 515 |
| 23707-2 | California, Here I Come | Com 515 |

Joe Bushkin plays a masterful solo on "California, Here I Come," one of the best piano choruses I've ever heard.

In December 1938 I recorded a parody of Noel Coward's *Private Lives* for Commodore. *Private Jives,* as it was called, was written by Johnny DeVries and read by Minerva Pious, Everett Sloane, and me. Joe Bushkin played trumpet and piano.

DUO RECORDING

Bud Freeman, ts; Jess Stacy, p
New York, June 13, 1939

| R-2126-2 | She's Funny That Way | Com 529 |

BUD FREEMAN AND HIS SUMMA CUM LAUDE ORCHESTRA

Max Kaminsky, tp; Brad Gowans, vtb; Pee Wee Russell, cl; Bud Freeman, ts; Dave Bowman, p; Eddie Condon, g; Clyde Newcomb, sb; Danny Alvin, d
New York, July 19, 1939

038291-1	I've Found a New Baby	Bl B-10370
038292-1	Easy to Get	Bl B-10370
038293-1	China Boy	Bl B-10386
038294-1	The Eel	Bl B-10386

This band used to rehearse all the time. I gave most if not all of the ideas to Brad, who was also our arranger, and he'd write them down. Danny Alvin was playing with us at Nick's Sizzling Steaks. Dave Tough had been playing with us but he took off on one of his drinking sprees. We always got Dave when we could have him, when he wasn't misbehaving. Lots of other bandleaders would take him whenever they could too. The best band

Woody Herman ever had was the one with Dave in it. He made that band what it was.

BUD FREEMAN AND HIS FAMOUS CHICAGOANS
    Jack Teagarden, tb & v; Pee Wee Russell, cl; Bud Freeman, ts; Dave Bowman, p; Eddie Condon, g; Mort Stuhlmaker, sb; Dave Tough, d
New York, July 23, 1940

27684-1	Jack Hits the Road	Col 35854
27685-1	47th and State	Col 35855

personnel: same as above except Max Kaminsky (t) added

| 27690-1 | After Awhile | Col 35856 |

Dave Tough played on this session and it was one of the finest pieces of drumming I've ever heard. All the avant-garde drummers today are influenced either directly or indirectly by his playing on the album. "Jack Hits the Road" is a composition of mine. I still get royalties on it. I told the A&R man at Columbia Records that I'd like to have Jack Teagarden on the session and he said, "Oh, I don't think you can have him, he's on the road with his orchestra." But Jack left his band to join us. In fact, he stayed up all night and came in and did the session, that's how much he wanted to do it. He said, "I came to see Bud Freeman. I came a long, long way. I thought for awhile I was on the road for MCA." So I called the tune "Jack Hits the Road." "47th and State" and "After Awhile" are also originals. I gave Benny Goodman "After Awhile" in the twenties and his firm still publishes it.

"STOP, LOOK AND LISTEN TO BUD FREEMAN"
    Reuben "Ruby" Brath, tp; Bud Freeman, ts; Kenny Kersey, p; Al Hall, sb; George Wettling, d
New York, July 1955
    Aff 112
    Stop, Look and Listen
    Newport News
    At Sundown
    Exactly Like You
    Let's Do It
    But Not for Me
    Dave's Blues
    Hapid
    "Newport News" is an original. So is "Hapid" and "Dave's Blues," which was named for Dave Bowman.

"SOMETHING TENDER"
Bud Freeman, ts; Karl Cress, g; George Barnes, g
New York, Apr. 1963
UA 15033 (S)
The Eel's Nephew
The Disenchanted Trout
The three of us were rehearsing and doing some club dates and I thought we ought to record. This is an excellent album, maybe the best I ever made. "The Eel's Nephew" and "The Disenchanted Trout" are both originals.

Index of Names

103 | Index of Names

ROBERT WOLF has a B.S. from Columbia University and an M.A. from the University of Chicago. He has been a schoolteacher, university lecturer, ranch hand, surveyor, dishwasher, and journalist. A playwright-in-residence for the San Quentin Drama Workshop, he was also dramaturge for Chicago's Organic Theater. He currently lives in Nashville and is completing a history of Chicago jazz.

Books in the Series Music in American Life

Only a Miner: Studies in Recorded Coal-Mining Songs
Archie Green

Great Day Coming: Folk Music and the American Left
R. Serge Denisoff

John Philip Sousa: A Descriptive Catalog of His Works
Paul E. Bierley

The Hell-Bound Train: A Cowboy Songbook
Glenn Ohrlin

Oh, Didn't He Ramble: The Life Story of Lee Collins
as Told to Mary Collins
Frank J. Gillis and John W. Miner, Editors

American Labor Songs of the Nineteenth Century
Philip S. Foner

Stars of Country Music:
Uncle Dave Macon to Johnny Rodriguez
Bill C. Malone and Judith McCulloh, Editors

Git Along, Little Dogies:
Songs and Songmakers of the American West
John I. White

A Texas-Mexican *Cancionero*: Folksongs of the Lower Border
Americo Paredes

San Antonio Rose: The Life and Music of Bob Wills
Charles R. Townsend

Early Downhome Blues: A Musical and Cultural Analysis
Jeff Todd Titon

An Ives Celebration: Papers and Panels of the Charles Ives
Centennial Festival-Conference
H. Wiley Hitchcock and Vivian Perlis, Editors

Sinful Tunes and Spirituals:
Black Folk Music to the Civil War
Dena J. Epstein

Joe Scott, the Woodsman-Songmaker
Edward D. Ives

Jimmie Rodgers:
The Life and Times of America's Blue Yodeler
Nolan Porterfield

Secular Music in Colonial Annapolis:
The Tuesday Club, 1745-56
John Barry Talley

Bibliographical Handbook of American Music
D. W. Krummel

Goin' to Kansas City
Nathan W. Pearson, Jr.

"Susanna," "Jeanie," and "The Old Folks at Home":
The Songs of Stephen C. Foster from His Time to Ours
SECOND EDITION
William W. Austin

Songprints:
The Musical Experience of Five Shoshone Women
Judith Vander

"Happy in the Service of the Lord":
Afro-American Gospel Quartets in Memphis
Kip Lornell

Paul Hindemith in the United States
Luther Noss

"My Song Is My Weapon":
People's Songs, American Communism, and the Politics of Culture
Robbie Lieberman

Chosen Voices: The Story of the American Cantorate
Mark Slobin

Theodore Thomas:
America's Conductor and Builder of Orchestras, 1835-1905
Ezra Schabas

"The Whorehouse Bells Were Ringing"
and Other Songs Cowboys Sing
Guy Logsdon

Crazeology:
The Autobiography of a Chicago Jazzman
Bud Freeman, as Told to Robert Wolf

Discoursing Sweet Music:
Town Bands and Community Life in Wayne County, Pennsylvania, 1897-1901
Kenneth Kreitner